OWN IT! 1

A2 Key test content in *Own It!* Level 1 has been checked by Cambridge Assessment English for accuracy and level.

STUDENT'S BOOK

WITH DIGITAL PACK

Claire Thacker
with Melissa Wilson and Daniel Vincent

CAMBRIDGE
UNIVERSITY PRESS

CONTENTS

5 WHAT'S YOUR STYLE?

LEARNING OUTCOMES

I can …

- understand texts about fashion and a Hindu wedding
- buy clothes and accessories
- write a description of a photo
- understand how to use present tenses
- talk about clothes and accessories
- make a picture dictionary and practise vocabulary by making connections.

Start it!

1 What is your style? Look at the photos. What do you like wearing?
2 Before you watch, which people wear uniforms?
3 Have all schools got uniforms? Watch and check.
4 Do you think uniforms are a good idea?

Watch video 5.1

p61

Language in action 5.2

p63

Language in action 5.3

p64

Everyday English 5.4

p66

Globetrotters 5.5

VOCABULARY
Clothes

5.01 **1 Match the words in the box with the pictures. Listen, check and repeat.**

boots	☐	cap	☐
hoodie	☐	jacket	☐
jeans	☐	joggers	☐
flip-flops	☐	trainers	☐
T-shirt	☐	skirt	☐
shirt	☐	shorts	*a*

2 Which look do you prefer? Why? Compare with a partner.

3 Circle the odd one out.

1 skirt / jeans / joggers / shorts
2 flip-flops / trainers / shirt / boots
3 shorts / jacket / hoodie
4 shirt / hoodie / jeans / T-shirt
5 jacket / cap / shirt / hoodie

LEARN TO LEARN
Making a picture dictionary

Drawing and labelling pictures helps you remember new words.

4 Make a picture dictionary for the clothes in Exercise 1. Compare with a partner.

5 Add more pictures to your dictionary. Cover the labels and show the pictures to a partner. Can they guess the words?

Use it!

6 Discuss the questions.

1 What do you wear to school / at the weekend?
2 What is your favourite outfit? Why?

Explore it!

Guess the correct answer.

Flip-flops have a lot of different names around the world. What do people in New Zealand call them?

a slops b jandals c chinelos

What do you call them? Find an interesting clothes fact. Write a question for your partner to answer.

READING
An online diary

1 Look at the photos and describe the clothes you see. Where do you think the people are from?

5.02 2 Read the online diary and check your answer to Exercise 1.

3 Choose the correct answer. Which person …

Michiko	Sofia	Akiko

1 has got a pet? Michiko
2 has got a maths test? ______
3 wants to go outside? ______
4 is Michiko's friend? ______
5 is wearing boots? ______
6 is wearing sandals? ______

4 Find adjectives in the online diary for the headings. Add two more adjectives for each heading.

Colour: black ______ ______ ______ ______ ______

Size: ______ ______ ______

Style: ______ ______ ______ ______ ______

Voice it!

5 Discuss the questions.

1 Do you dress like your friends? Why / Why not?
2 How do the people you like influence the clothes you wear?
3 How does the place you live in influence the clothes you wear?

Finished? p122 Ex 1

Michiko's Mix.com

Saturday, 8 am
HAPPY WEEKEND!

I'm writing this post in my bedroom. My cat, Candy, is sleeping right here beside me.

What are you doing this morning? It's so hot!

Comments:

10 replies ❤ 12 likes

Sofia: Hi, Michiko. I'm revising for a maths test! ☹ It's really hot and I want to be outside!

Michiko: Poor you! Good luck! My friend is calling me. See you later!

10 AM (and back online!)
We ❤ Harajuku – the fashion district

I'm sitting in a café with my best friend, Akiko. We're mixing traditional Japanese clothes with our own clothes to create a wamono style today. Look! We're wearing summer dresses and shirts. I'm wearing big black boots but Akiko isn't wearing the same boots. She's wearing zori (they're Japanese sandals).

We're also people watching from the café! There are a lot of different looks. There's a boy outside the café. He's wearing a black and white striped T-shirt, a red shirt, tight jeans, a green jacket and trainers. What a cool retro sporty look! What do you think?

Comments:

Kyle from London: I love it!

1 PM Lunchtime

I'm not having ramen today. I've got sushi and sashimi. It's definitely a susimi kind of day. Delicious! Are you having ramen for lunch?

Comments:

Lily: No, I'm not. I'm making pizza for ten friends!

Watch video 5.2
What is he wearing?
Is Hiro wearing a uniform?

LANGUAGE IN ACTION
Present continuous

I	he/she/it	we/you/they
I [1] *'m* *writing* this post in my bedroom.	Akiko **is wearing** Japanese sandals.	We [2] _____ _____ traditional Japanese clothes.
I [3] _____ _____ _____ ramen today.	Akiko [4] _____ _____ black boots.	Michiko and Akiko **aren't wearing** the same boots.
[5] _____ I _____ this in my bedroom?	**Is** Sofia **revising** this morning?	What **are** you **doing** this morning? [6] _____ you _____ ramen for lunch?
Yes, I **am**. / No, I**'m not**.	Yes, **she is**. / No, **she isn't**.	Yes, I **am**. / No, I [7] _____ _____.

Pronunciation p142

1 **Complete the examples in the table above. Use the online diary on page 60 to help you.**

2 **Complete the posts with the present continuous form of the verbs.**

What [1] *are* you *doing* (do)?

I [2] _____ (draw) my own design on my T-shirt. I [3] _____ (create) my own style. 🙂 *Emy*

I [4] _____ (not sit) on the beach today because it [5] _____ (rain) but I [6] _____ (wear) flip-flops.
Felipe

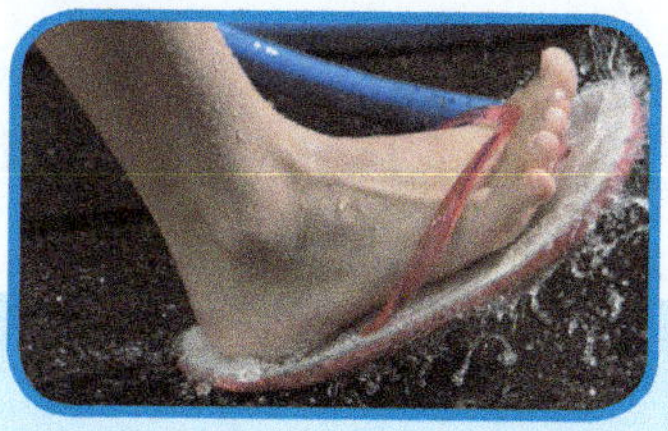

I [7] _____ (not wear) flip-flops but that's a good idea! *Sergio*

3 **Remember the information from the online diary. Write sentences in the present continuous. Check with a partner. How many sentences have you got?**

Get it right!

We say: *Are you wearing a cap?* **NOT** ~~*You are wearing a cap?*~~

4 **Choose a classmate but don't tell your partner. Ask questions to guess your partner's classmate. Ask ten questions. Your partner can only answer *Yes* or *No*!**

Is this person sitting near me? — *No.*

Use it!

5 **Write present continuous questions. Ask and answer with a partner.**

1 what / you / wear / today?
_____

2 which TV series / you / watch / this month? _____
_____

3 where / your best friend / sit?
_____

4 what / you / think about / right now?
_____

What are you wearing today?

I'm wearing my favourite jeans, but I'm not wearing flip-flops.

Finished? p122 Ex 2

VOCABULARY AND LISTENING

Accessories

5.05 **1 Match the words with the photos. Listen, check and repeat.**

belt	☐	bracelet	☐	earrings	☐
gloves	☐	necklace	☐	purse	1
ring	☐	scarf	☐	sunglasses	☐
umbrella	☐	wallet	☐	watch	☐

2 Write the words from Exercise 1 in the correct place in the table.

Carry	purse		
Wear	belt		

Use it!

3 Work with a partner. Ask and answer.

Which of the accessories in Exercise 1 …

1 are you wearing/carrying today?
2 have you got at home?
3 do you wear/carry every day?

An interview

4 Look at the photos. What are the people wearing? Do you like the clothes?

LEARN TO LEARN

Listening for the general idea

When you listen for the first time, don't worry if you don't understand every word. Listen for the general idea.

5.06 **5 Listen to the interview. What is Tom talking about?**

a his family   b his job   c his clothes

5.06 **6 Listen again. Are the sentences *T* (true) or *F* (false)? Correct the false sentences.**

Tom …

1 designs clothes for musicians. ___
2 usually starts work at 7 am. ___
3 never works late. ___
4 is good at drawing. ___
5 makes the clothes. ___

LANGUAGE IN ACTION
Present simple and present continuous

Watch video 5.3
Which clothes and accessories do you hear? Which three tips does she give?

Present simple (facts, habits and routines)	Present continuous (things happening now)
I **design** clothes for TV actors.	Today [1]I'm ______ **finishing** the designs.
I **don't make** the clothes.	Emily **isn't making** a shirt.
What [2]______ you **do**?	What [3]______ she **making** now?
I[4]______ a costume designer.	She[5]______ **making** a skirt and a belt.
Time expressions: adverbs of frequency, days of the week, every day	Time expressions: now, just now, right now, today, this morning/week/month/year, at the moment

1 **Complete the examples in the table above.**

2 **Match 1–5 with a–e. Compare with a partner.**

1 Tom is working on a TV series
2 Tom starts work
3 Tom is designing
4 Emily makes
5 Emily is making

a all the clothes.
b a skirt and a belt today.
c the girls' outfits today.
d at 7 am every day.
e at the moment.

5.07 **3** **Complete the blog post with the present simple or present continuous form of the verbs in brackets. Listen and check.**

[1] Do you want (want) to know more about my life?

What [2]______ we ______ (do) this week?

We [3]______ (study) the history of fashion in art. It's really interesting and I [4]______ (learn) lots of cool new stuff.
We [5]______ (prepare) our class fashion show this week, too. Joe and I [6]______ (wear) clothes from the 1980s. We [7]______ usually ______ (not wear) clothes like this. We [8]______ (not smile) in the photo but we like the look! I ♥ [9]______ (love) the 1980s.

What [10]______ you ______ (do) right now?

Post a comment:

Use it!

4 **Write questions with the present simple or present continuous. Ask and answer.**

What …

1 you / always / wear / at the weekend?
What do you always wear at the weekend?

2 music / you / listen to / at the moment?
______

Who …

3 you / sit next to / right now?
______

4 you / usually sit next to / at lunchtime?
______

What do you always wear at the weekend?

I always wear joggers on Saturday and jeans on Sunday.

Finished? p122 Ex 3

SPEAKING
Buying clothes or accessories

1 Look at the photo. What do you think Salif wants to buy?

5.08 2 Listen to the conversation. Does Salif find what he's looking for?

SALES ASSISTANT Good afternoon. [1]Can I help you?
SALIF Yes, please. [2]__________ a scarf for my grandma.
SA Sure. Let's have a look. [3]__________
SALIF My grandma doesn't wear pink. [4]__________ a different colour?
SA Yes, I have. You're in luck! [5]__________ blue or purple.
SALIF [6]__________ the purple one, please?
SA Here you go. What do you think?
SALIF It's perfect. How much is it?
SA It's £8 but there's a special offer today. Buy two for £12.
SALIF No, thanks. I'm fine with just one!
SA Are you sure? It's a bargain.
SALIF No, honestly. One is fine.

5.08 3 Complete the conversation with phrases from the *Useful language* box. Listen and check.

Useful language

Can I help you?
Can I see the … one, please?
Have you got it in a different (size/colour/style)?
I'm looking for …
It comes in …
What about this one / these?

4 Look at the *Everyday English* box. Find and underline the phrases in the conversation.

5 Work with a partner. Practise the conversation.

Watch video 5.4
Everyday English

It's a bargain. It's perfect.
No, honestly. You're in luck!

PLAN

6 Work in pairs. Decide who is the customer and who is the sales assistant.

CUSTOMER Decide what you are buying and who it is for. Use the ideas below or your own ideas.

something new to wear to a party
new earrings for your friend's birthday
some new trainers for yourself

SALES ASSISTANT Think about different colours and sizes, prices and special offers.

SPEAK

7 Practise the conversation about buying something with your partner. Remember to use the present simple and present continuous, the vocabulary from this unit and expressions from the *Useful language* and *Everyday English* boxes.

CHECK

8 Work with another pair. Listen to their conversation and complete the notes.

What does the customer buy?
____
How much is it?
____
Was it a special offer?
____

WRITING
A description of a photo

1 **Look at the photo. Which person is Emin? Read the description and find the answer.**

My favourite photo By Emin

1 ☐ This is a photo of my friends and me. We're all sitting on the beach. We're celebrating my friend Irem's 13th birthday.

2 ☐ Irem and I are in the middle. She's wearing a white T-shirt and a woollen jacket. She's laughing. My friend Greg is on the left. Greg's wearing a red checked shirt. He usually wears a cap but he isn't wearing it in this photo. He's holding some food but he isn't eating. Sophie is next to Greg. She's wearing her new jeans. My friend Hakan is on the right. He's wearing his favourite checked shirt and his new trainers. He's smiling. There isn't anyone at the back in this photo. I'm next to Hakan. I'm wearing beige trousers and a grey hoodie, with a white T-shirt under it because it's cold.

3 ☐ This is my favourite photo because I'm with my friends and we're all having a great time.

2 **Read the description again and answer the questions.**

1 What are they celebrating?

____

2 Where are they?

____

3 What is Irem wearing?

____

4 What does Greg usually wear?

____

5 Why does Emin like this photo?

____

____

3 **Match topics a–c with paragraphs 1–3.**

a Description of the people in the photo.
b Brief description of who is in the photo.
c Opinion on why it is your favourite photo.

4 **Complete the expressions in the *Useful language* box.**

Useful language

[1] at the back	[4] ______ the right
[2] ______ the middle	next [5] ______ (someone)
on [3] ______ left	

Write your own description of a photo.

PLAN

5 **Look at the photo below and make notes. Decide what information to include in each paragraph of the description. Use the information in Exercise 3 to help you.**

WRITE

6 **Write your description. Remember to include the information in the correct order, the present simple and present continuous, and expressions from the *Useful language* box.**

CHECK

7 **Do you …**

- describe people in the photo, including the clothes and accessories they are wearing?
- describe the people's positions in the photo?
- say why you like the photo?

Finished? p122 Ex 4

AROUND THE WORLD

READING
A magazine article interview

1 Look at the photo of the people. Discuss the questions.

1. Where do you think they are from?
2. What do you think they are celebrating?
3. What is the woman at the front holding?

5.09 **2 Read the interview and check your answers to Exercise 1.**

3 Read the interview again and answer the questions.

1. How long does a Hindu wedding last for?
______
2. What is a lehenga?
______
3. What colour is popular for Hindu weddings? Why?
______
4. What accessories is Mishal wearing in the photo?
______
5. What is a sherwani?
______

4 Complete the table with adjectives ending in *-ful* from the interview. Check the meanings in a dictionary.

Noun	Adjective
1 wonder	wonderful
2 colour	
3 beauty	
4 power	

Globetrotters
Watch video 5.5
Culture and Fashion

- Where do the 'blue people' live?
- What do the Sami make?
- Which colour is important for the Maasai?

Special Days

Weddings are a wonderful time for families and friends to celebrate together and to wear special clothes. This week, Amrit is talking about his cousin's Hindu wedding in India and some of their traditions.

Q: What are Hindu weddings like?
A: They're incredible! There's a lot of amazing food, music and dancing. They're always very colourful events because everyone wears beautiful clothes. They last for three days.

Q: What does the bride wear?

A: The bride usually wears a lehenga (a long skirt with a top) and a long scarf. Red is very popular at Hindu weddings. It's a powerful colour because in India it symbolises love and new life. In this photo, my cousin Mishal is wearing a red and gold lehenga. She's also wearing special wedding accessories: a gold necklace, earrings, rings on her fingers and toes, and lots of red and gold bracelets.

Q: What does the groom wear?

A: The groom usually wears a sherwani (a long jacket with gold designs on it), a pair of trousers and special wedding shoes. My cousin's new husband, Ranjit, is also wearing a red turban.

Q: Are there are any other special wedding traditions?

A: There are lots, but my favourite is joota chupai – a member of the bride's family steals the groom's wedding shoes and hides them. It's great fun! In this photo, my aunt Jaz is holding Ranjit's shoes and everyone is laughing.

People around the world celebrate special days like weddings and birthdays in different ways. How do you celebrate special days in your country?

Voice it!

5 **Answer the questions.**

1 What do people wear to special celebrations in your country?

2 What is a typical wedding like in your country?

3 Are colours important in your country? Have they got special meanings?

LEARN TO LEARN

Making connections (2)

When you read an article, try to make connections with your own life and experiences. This can help you to understand the article more easily.

6 **Think about a special celebration in your life and answer the questions.**

1 Is there a part of this article that reminds you of that special celebration?

2 Who and what does it remind you of: people, food, clothes, traditions?

7 **Explain your connections to your partner. Are your partner's connections the same or different?**

Explore it!

Guess the correct answer.

Hindu brides have special paint on their hands. What does the design include?

a their age b their husband's name

c their favourite food

Find out about other interesting Hindu wedding traditions. Choose your favourite tradition and write a question for your partner to answer.

OWN IT! The Culture Project Teacher's Resource Bank

5 REVIEW

VOCABULARY

1 Complete the names of clothes with the missing vowels.

1 j _ _ ns
2 tr _ _ n _ rs
3 sh _ rt
4 b _ _ ts
5 h _ _ d _ _
6 sh _ rts
7 c _ p
8 j _ gg _ rs

2 Write the accessories.

1 two things you can wear on your wrist
_______ _______
2 two things you can put your money in
_______ _______
3 something you can use when it's raining
____
4 things you can wear in your ears
____
5 things you can wear on your hands when it's cold _______

3 Look at the pictures. What are they wearing? Write the clothes and accessories.

1 _______
2 _______
3 _______
4 _______
5 _______
6 _______
7 _______
8 _______

LANGUAGE IN ACTION

4 Complete the conversations. Use the correct form of the present continuous.

1 you / watch / TV just now?
✗ do / my homework
____
____

2 Lidia / wear / a red T-shirt today?
✗ wear / a blue shirt
____
____

3 Mike / chat / with his friends at the moment?
✗ take / a photo
____
____

5 Complete the posts with the present simple or present continuous form of the verbs.

What [1] _______ you usually _______ (wear) at school?

I usually [2] _______ (wear) jeans and a T-shirt. It [3] _______ (rain) today so I [4] _______ (carry) an umbrella!

[5] _______ your dad _______ (work) today?

No, he [6] _______ (not work) on Saturdays. He often [7] _______ (play) football, but today he [8] _______ (not do) that. He and Mum [9] _______ (shop) in Hull.

Self-assessment

I can name twelve clothes words in English.

I can name twelve accessories in English.

I can use the present continuous to talk about what is happening now.

I can use the present simple and the present continuous together.

LEARN TO LEARN

LEARN TO ... GUESS THE MEANING OF WORDS

When you don't know a word, you can guess the meaning. This helps you to read and listen in English.

1 Circle the answer that is true for you. Compare and discuss your answer with a partner.

When I see a word I don't know, I usually ...

1. guess the meaning.
2. ask the teacher what it means.
3. look in a dictionary.
4. write it in my notebook.

2 Read the text. Discuss the questions about each of the words in bold with a partner.

I don't like tight jeans. I prefer **baggy** jeans because they're comfortable. I have lots of T-shirts, T-shirts with long **sleeves**, T-shirts with short **sleeves**, but I don't like T-shirts with **logos** – I don't like pictures or writing on my clothes. I love trainers. I have big feet so it can be difficult to find my size, but my new trainers **fit** really well. They're the perfect size!

1 Are they nouns, verbs or adjectives?

I think 'baggy' is an adjective.

2 What clues about the meaning can you find in the text?

Baggy jeans are not tight.
Baggy jeans are comfortable.

3 What do you think each of the words in **bold** means?

I think 'baggy' means not tight.

OWN IT!

3 Read the text. Answer the questions in Exercise 2 about each of the words in bold.

I never wear rings, bracelets or earrings, because I don't like **jewellery**, but I have lots of hats, gloves and scarves. Why? Well, my grandma loves to make me clothes – she especially loves to **knit** me clothes. I'm happy about this, because I like to be **warm** on cold winter days, and woollen clothes are great for that!

jewellery

1 noun ____________________

2 ____________________

____

3 ____________________

knit

1 ____________________

2 ____________________

____

3 ____________________

warm

1 ____________________

2 ____________________

____

3 ____________________

6 SPORT FOR LIFE

LEARNING OUTCOMES

I can ...

- understand texts about sport
- book tickets
- write a profile
- understand how to use comparatives and superlatives
- talk about sports
- say collocations out loud and remember vocabulary sets together
- make an information leaflet.

Start it!

1. Look at the photo. What do you think these people are doing?
2. Before you watch, guess three sports from the video.
3. Which other sports can you see? Watch and check.
4. Which sport do you want to try? Why?

Watch video 6.1

p73

Language in action 6.2

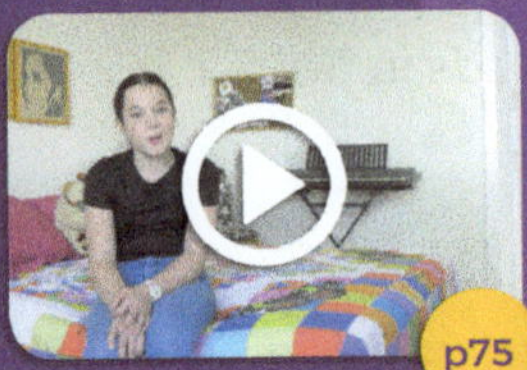

p75

Language in action 6.3

p76

Everyday English 6.4

VOCABULARY
Sports

6.01 **1 Match the words in the box with the photos. Listen, check and repeat.**

athletics	☐	basketball	☐
(mountain/rock) climbing			☐
gymnastics	☐	hockey	☐
rugby	☐	running	☐
sailing	☐	swimming	☐
table tennis	a	volleyball	☐
windsurfing	☐	yoga	☐

6.02 **2 Listen. Which six sports do you hear?**

1 *table tennis* ________ 4 ________
2 ________ 5 ________
3 ________ 6 ________

LEARN TO LEARN
Saying collocations out loud

When you learn new collocations, say the words out loud. There are three main verbs we use with sports.

play	ball sports
go	sports that end in *-ing*
do	other sports

3 Write the sports from Exercise 1 in the spidergram. Say them out loud as you write them. How many more sports can you add?

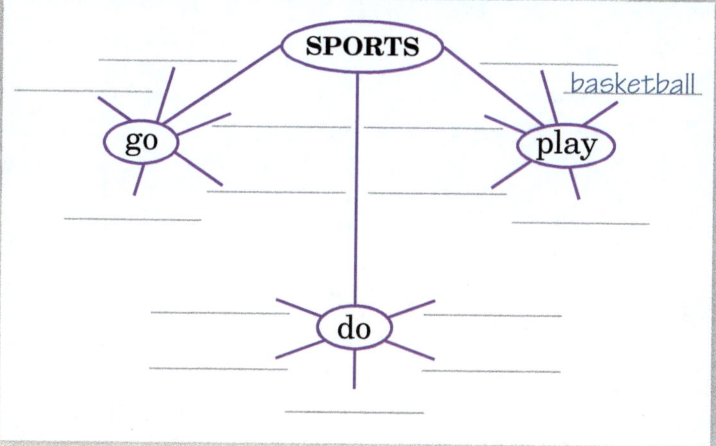

4 Work in pairs. Say a sport out loud and your partner says the verb.

Use it!

5 Discuss the questions.

1 Which sports do you do? How often do you do them?
2 Do you prefer team sports or individual sports? Why?
3 Which sports do you want to try?

Explore it!

Guess the correct answer.

Tennis star Serena Williams wears … every day during a tennis tournament.

a a lucky necklace b different trainers
c the same socks

Find an interesting fact about a sport. Write a question for your partner to answer.

READING

Online FAQs

1 **What do you think the people in the photo are doing? Tell your partner.**

6.03 **2** **Read the article. Match the questions with the answers in the FAQs.**

3 **Read the article again. Are the sentences *T* (true) or *F* (false)?**

1 A bossaball team has a maximum of five people. T
2 Players can't use their feet. ___
3 A bossaball ball is the same size as a football. ___
4 You can play bossaball when it's raining. ___
5 The inventor of bossaball isn't a DJ. ___

4 **Find the meaning of the words in bold in the FAQs. Are they positive or negative? Can you add any more adjectives?**

Positive	Negative
amazing	

Voice it!

5 **Discuss the questions.**

1 Can you play bossaball in your town?
2 Do you think bossaball looks interesting or boring? Why?
3 Do you want to try it?

Finished? p123 Ex 1

Bossaball

Do you need some help? You can't decide? What do you play: volleyball or football or maybe gymnastics? Don't worry! We've got the answer – you can do all of them. Bossaball is the answer!

FAQs

Q1: What is it?
Q2: Is it a team game?
Q3: Where can I play it?
Q4: How big is a bossaball?
Q5: Can players touch the ball?
Q6: Is there an age limit?

Answers

A1: It's almost the same size as a volleyball and smaller than a football.
A2: No, there isn't. It's suitable for people of all ages.
A3: Yes, it is. There are two teams and each team has three, four or five players.
A4: Yes, they can. Players can use their hands and arms or their feet.
A5: It's a mixture of football, volleyball and gymnastics with music. It's more **entertaining** than other ball sports and in some places it's becoming more **popular** than beach volleyball.
A6: You can play it indoors if the weather's **bad**, but people usually play outdoors in a park or on a beach.

Bossaball players think it's better than volleyball and it's more **exciting** than football. It definitely isn't **boring** to watch and it's even more **amazing** to play. What are you waiting for?

The inventor of Bossaball is Filip Eyckmans – he's Belgian. His favourite sports are tennis and football and he also loves music and dance. In fact, he's a DJ. Bossaball is a combination of his favourite things and it's great fun!

LANGUAGE IN ACTION

Comparatives

Watch video 6.2
Which sports does he talk about?
Which sport is healthy?

Comparative adjectives		
Short adjectives	**Long adjectives**	**Irregular adjectives**
A bossaball is [1] _smaller_ than a football.	It's **more exciting** than football.	It's [2] ________ than volleyball.
A football is **bigger** than a bossaball.	Bossaball is becoming [3] ________ ________ than beach volleyball.	The weather is **worse** today than yesterday.

Pronounciation p142

1 **Complete the examples in the table above. Use the article on page 72 to help you.**

2 **Write the comparative form of the adjectives.**

1 bad _worse_
2 big ________
3 boring ________
4 fast ________
5 good ________
6 tall ________

3 **Complete the sentences with the comparative form of the adjectives. Check your answers in the article on page 72.**

big ~~entertaining~~
exciting good

1 Bossaball is _more entertaining than_ other ball sports.
2 Bossaball is ________ football.
3 A football is ________ a bossaball or a volleyball.
4 Do you think bossaball is ________ other sports you know?

4 **Write sentences with the comparative form of the adjectives. Use the correct form of the verb *be*.**

1 windsurfing (exciting) swimming
Windsurfing is more exciting than swimming.
2 table tennis (interesting) yoga
____
3 climbing (difficult) volleyball
____
4 basketball players (tall) football players
____
____

Use it!

5 **Write sentences to compare some of the things below or use your own ideas. Use adjectives from the box or think of your own. Discuss with a partner. Do you agree?**

boring comfortable difficult easy exciting
good healthy interesting smart tasty

table tennis / tennis
hanging out with friends / going shopping
Italian food / Indian food
joggers / jeans

I think table tennis is more interesting than tennis. What do you think?

I don't agree. I think tennis is more interesting.

Finished? p123 Ex 2

1 throw / dive / pass

2 kick / hit / jump

3 catch / lift / bounce

4 climb / run / score

VOCABULARY AND LISTENING

Sports verbs

6.06 **1 Circle the correct verb to describe the photos. Listen, repeat and check. Can you guess the meaning of the other verbs?**

Get it right!

You **win** or **lose** a game, match, race or competition.

When you win, you **beat** the person or people you are competing with.

I want to win the race. **NOT** ~~*I want to beat the race.*~~

I think we can beat this team. **NOT** ~~*I think we can win this team.*~~

6.07 **2 Circle the correct verbs. Can you guess the sports? Listen and check.**

This is a popular team sport in Asia. It's a combination of volleyball and football. Players can't use their hands. One player [1]*dives* / *passes* the ball to another player to start. Players [2]*run* / *kick* the ball with their feet. The first team to [3]*throw* / *score* 21 points in two games wins.

a capoeira

b underwater hockey

c sepak takraw

This is a team game with six soft balls. It's popular in PE classes in the UK. Players [4]*lift* / *run* fast to pick up balls from the middle of the court. Then they [5]*dive* / *throw* their balls at the other team. If a ball [6]*hits* / *jumps* someone, that person is 'out'. Players can [7]*catch* / *score* a ball in their hands, but if it [8]*climbs* / *bounces* off another player, they can't use it.

a basketball

b dodgeball

c volleyball

LEARN TO LEARN

Remembering vocabulary sets

Think about which verbs you can use for each sport.

3 Work with a partner and add other verbs to the diagram.

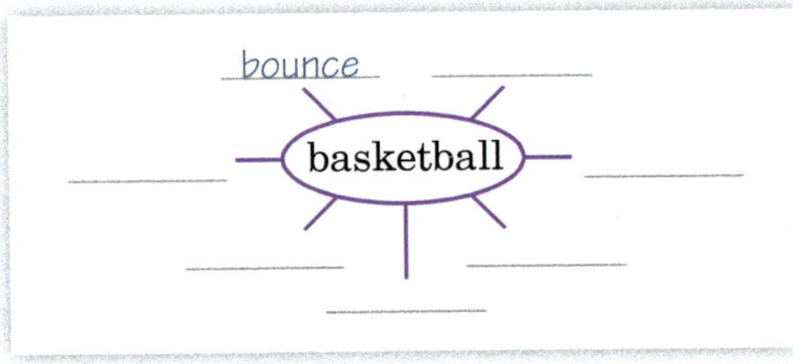

Use it!

4 Choose a sport and describe it in three sentences. Use verbs from Exercise 1. Can your partner guess the sport?

A conversation

6.08 **5 Look at the photos. Why do you think these people are famous? Listen and check.**

Johanna Quaas

Sun Ming Ming

6.08 **6 Listen again. Circle the correct answers.**

1 Johanna Quaas trains for an hour every ....

a week b day c morning

2 She doesn't eat much ....

a meat b fruit c meat or fruit

3 Sun Ming Ming's trainers are size ....

a 41 b 55 c 37

4 Sun Ming Ming and his wife are both very ....

a popular b tall c old

LANGUAGE IN ACTION

Superlatives

Watch video 6.3
Who is the most amazing painter?
Who can play the piano?

Superlative adjectives		
Short adjectives	**Long adjectives**	**Irregular adjectives**
Has Sun Ming Ming got the **biggest** feet in the world?	The article is about some of the **most amazing** sportspeople in the world.	Fruit and vegetables are the **best** things to eat.

1 Look at the table above. Complete the sentences with the superlative form of the adjectives.

Johnna Quaas is ¹ the oldest (old) active gymnast in the world. She's probably ² ________ (fit) and ³ ________ (healthy) person in their 90s in the world.

Sun Ming Ming is ⁴ ________ (tall) basketball player in the world. Does the article say he is ⁵ ________ (good) player in his team?

2 Complete the sports quiz with the superlative form of the adjectives. Predict and circle the answers to the questions. Discuss with a partner.

6.09 **3 Listen and check your answers to Exercise 2.**

THE BIGGEST (BIG) SPORTS QUIZ IN THE WORLD!

1 Fauja Singh is over 100 and he's very active. He's ________ (old) person to *run a marathon / climb Mount Everest.*

2 Juju Noda hasn't got a car but she can drive. She is ________ (young) person to drive an *F4 / F1* racing car.

3 Many people say that *basketball / football* is ________ (easy) sport to learn to play.

4 ________ (fast) time for the men's 100 m race at an Olympic Games is *9.58 / 9* seconds.

5 *Volleyball / Table tennis* is ________ (popular) indoor sport. People of all ages play it. You only need a net, a ball and a bat.

6 ________ (good) food to eat before you do sport or exercise is a *carrot / banana.*

Use it!

4 Write four sentences with your opinions about sports. Use the words in boxes A and B. Compare with a partner. Do you agree?

A
easiest most boring
most difficult
most interesting on TV

B
do learn play watch

5 Write sentences with superlative adjectives about you. Use the topics in the box or choose your own topics. Ask and answer with a partner.

day of the week (good)
food (delicious)
sportsperson (amazing)
person (happy)

Which is the best day of the week?

I think Friday is the best day of the week because I always finish school early. What about you?

Finished? p123 Ex 3

SPEAKING

Buying tickets online

6.10 **1 Listen to the conversation. How much do they pay for the tickets?**

6.10 **2 Complete the conversation with the phrases from the *Useful language* box. Listen and check.**

Useful language

How much are tickets?
Let's go.
They're (£45).
Let's book them.
Shall we go?
What's the (quickest/best/cheapest) way to get there?

3 Look at the *Everyday English* box. Find and underline the phrases in the conversation.

Watch video 6.4
Everyday English

Got them! Look! That's crazy!
What are we waiting for? Why not?

4 Work with a partner. Practise the conversation.

RUBEN Look! Our favourite team is playing football this afternoon. [1] Shall we go ________?
OMAR Why not? [2] ________
RUBEN The best seats are the most expensive. [3] ________.
OMAR That's crazy! Are there any cheaper tickets?
RUBEN Yes, there are. The cheapest tickets are £12 but they're the worst seats.
OMAR That's OK. I don't mind if you don't. [4] ________.
RUBEN Got them! We collect and pay for them when we get there. The match starts in an hour.
OMAR What are we waiting for? [5] ________.
RUBEN [6] ________.
OMAR Run – fast!
RUBEN Wait for me!

PLAN

5 Work with a partner. Plan a conversation about buying tickets online for a sports event. Decide ...

what event you want to see.

a basketball game | a tennis match | an athletics event

____

how much the tickets cost.

____

how you are going to get there.

____

SPEAK

6 Practise the conversation with your partner. Remember to use comparatives and superlatives, the vocabulary from this unit and expressions from the *Useful language* and *Everyday English* boxes.

CHECK

7 Work with another pair. Listen to their conversation and complete the notes.

What event do they want to see?

____

How much are the tickets?

____

How are they going to get there?

____

WRITING

A profile of a sportsperson

1 **Look at the photo. What sport do you think Ashima Shiraishi does? Read Kelly's profile and check.**

2 **Match topics a–c with paragraphs 1–3.**

a Achievements

b Basic information and description

c Training and other interests

3 **Read the profile again and write two pieces of information for the paragraphs in Exercise 2.**

Achievements: first woman to climb the 'Horizon' rock

____

____

4 **Read the *Useful language* box and circle the correct words.**

Useful language

We use *also* and *too* to give extra information.

We use ***also*** [1]*before* / *after* the verb *be*.

We use ***also*** [2]*before* / *after* other verbs.

We use ***too*** at the [3]*beginning* / *end* of a sentence.

5 **Rewrite the second sentence with the word in brackets.**

1 I like playing football. I enjoy hanging out with friends. (also)

____

2 Table tennis is easy to play. It's fun. (too)

____

3 She's running. She's jumping. (also)

____

4 He's wearing new trainers. He's wearing a new T-shirt. (too)

____

My favourite sportsperson

By Kelly Nammour

1 ☐ My favourite sportsperson is Ashima Shiraishi. She's an American rock climber. She's 154 cm tall, she weighs 40 kg and she's smaller and lighter than most climbers. She lives in New York.

2 ☐ She trains five days a week after school with her father, Hisatoshi. He's also her coach. Ashima goes rock climbing whenever she can and she practises on climbing walls in the gym, too. She loves climbing but she also enjoys watching basketball on TV, listening to music and watching films.

3 ☐ I think she's amazing because she is the first woman and the youngest person to climb the 'Horizon' rock in Japan. It's one of the most difficult rocks in the world to climb. She is one of the world's strongest climbers and one of the most successful young sportspeople in the world too.

Write a profile of your favourite sportsperson.

PLAN

6 **Make notes about your favourite sportsperson. Decide what information to include in each paragraph. Use the information in Exercise 2 to help you.**

WRITE

7 **Write your description. Remember to incluse three paragraphs, comparatives and superlatives and expressions from the *Useful language* box.**

CHECK

8 **Do you …**

- give basic information and a description of your sportsperson?
- describe their sport using sports verbs?
- talk about their achievements and why you like them?

Finished? p123 Ex 4

THE PE PROJECT

An information leaflet

1 Look quickly at the leaflet. Circle its purpose.

1 to give directions to a sports club
2 to give information about a sport
3 to give transport times

2 Read the leaflet and make notes on the ideas in the box.

What?	When?	Where?	Who?
Equipment	One of the rules	One of the benefits	

3 Read the leaflet again. Are the sentences *T* (true) or *F* (false)?

1 You need some special equipment to play streetball. F
2 There are sometimes ten players in a game of streetball. ___
3 You can't touch the ball with your hands in streetball. ___
4 Some sports are more expensive than streetball. ___

How to design a leaflet

4 Read the tips about designing a leaflet. Circle the ones you think are good pieces of advice.

a Use serious colours, not bright ones.
b Use photos and a map.
c Make sure the people are not smiling in the photos.
d Include contact details.
e Choose a clear font (if you're using a computer) or write neatly.
f Include everything you know about the sport.

6.11 **5 Listen to the advice and check your answers to Exercise 4.**

STREETBALL

WHAT IS IT?

It's outdoor basketball in your local area.

WHERE AND WHEN?

We meet every Tuesday at 5.30 pm at the West Avenue basketball court. Come along and join us.

Find us here:

WHO?

Everyone is welcome! You don't need to belong to a team and you don't need special training.

WHY NOT COME ALONG AND MAKE NEW FRIENDS?

Equipment

We've got a basketball and nets. Just bring yourself and your trainers!

Teams

- A team can play with only two players but there are never more than five.

Rules

Different streetball games have different rules, but these are ours:

- Players can bounce, throw and catch the ball.
- When you score, your team gets one point.
- After you score, your team keeps the ball.
- A team wins when they score 7 points.

BENEFITS

- It's free!
- It's a great way to get fitter and healthier!
- The matches are faster and more exciting than normal basketball.
- It's great fun!

Any questions?
Contact Greg at gregscott@jmail.com.

FACT

Bucharest is the unofficial streetball capital of the world! Every year more than 1,000 streetball players travel to the Romanian capital city and play in a streetball competition.

PLAN

6 **Work with a group. Choose a street sport or another sport and find out information about it. Complete the steps below.**

- Decide on the information you want to include.
- Decide and choose the photos and illustrations to include.
- Draw a rough plan of the layout of the leaflet.
- Make a first draft of your leaflet.
- Discuss how you can improve your first draft.

PRESENT

7 **Prepare your final leaflet and present it to the class. Remember to include facts about your sport, photos, illustrations and maps, and the tips in *How to* design a leaflet.**

CHECK

8 **Look at your classmates' leaflets and complete the notes.**

Which sport is the most interesting?

____

Which leaflet has the best design?

____

Which sport do you want to try? Why?

____

____

6 REVIEW

VOCABULARY

1 Complete the sentences with the sports in the box.

mountain climbing | rugby | sailing | table tennis | volleyball | windsurfing | yoga

1 You need a net to play ________________ and ________________.

2 ________________ is a ball game that people always play outdoors.

3 People usually do ________________ indoors.

4 You need to be on the water to go ________________ or ________________.

5 ________________ can be dangerous, so you need very good equipment.

2 Circle the correct verbs.

1 We're playing football so we can *kick* / *score* the ball.

2 That looks heavy. Can you *climb* / *lift* it?

3 I want to *run* / *dive* a marathon one day.

4 *Catch* / *Throw* me that ball, please.

5 How do you *jump* / *score* in hockey?

6 It's important to *pass* / *hit* the ball in rugby.

LANGUAGE IN ACTION

3 Write the comparative form of the adjectives.

1 bad ________________

2 big ________________

3 easy ________________

4 exciting ________________

5 good ________________

6 interesting ________________

4 Look at the information and write sentences. Use comparative and superlative adjectives.

	Jack's opinion		
	Table tennis 	Rugby 	Hockey 
easy	★★★★★	★★	★
exciting	★	★★★★	★★
good	★★	★★★★	★

1 table tennis / easy

____

2 rugby / easy / hockey

____

3 hockey / exciting / table tennis

____

4 table tennis / good / hockey

____

5 rugby / good

____

6 rugby / exciting

____

Self-assessment

I can name thirteen sports in English.

I can use twelve sports verbs to talk about sports.

I can use comparative adjectives to compare two things.

I can use superlative adjectives to compare three or more things.

LEARN TO … WRITE EXAMPLE SENTENCES

Example sentences help you understand and remember vocabulary

1 **Read Peiyu's blog. How does she remember new words? Why?**

https:\\peiyusenglishlearningblog.co.uk

Today's tip

Peiyu's English learning blog

Remembering new words

When I learn new words, I use them in example sentences. I think this is better than writing them in my language. When I write sentences, I think about what the word means and this helps me to remember it.

Also, when you write example sentences, the meaning is easier to remember later because the other words in the sentence can help you. I try to write funny sentences or sentences about me and my friends because it's easier to remember the sentences.

Look at my notebook! What do you think?

My parents **do yoga** in the garden.

I **run** to school when I'm late.

2 **Circle the example sentences you prefer, a or b. Compare your answers with a partner and say why.**

1 bananas

a Bananas are nice.

(b) Bananas are a long yellow fruit.

I prefer example sentence b because the words 'long', 'yellow' and 'fruit' help you remember what bananas are.

2 kick

a In football, players kick a ball.

b They kick it.

3 rugby

a Rugby is my grandma's favourite sport.

b Rugby is boring.

4 throw

a Throw it!

b My baby sister throws her food at me.

OWN IT!

3 **Write an example sentence for each of the words in the box.**

beat catch rock climbing score volleyball

1 ______

2 ______

3 ______

4 ______

5 ______

4 **Tell your partner your sentences from Exercise 3. Who has the best example sentence for each word?**

I prefer your sentence for 'beat' because it's funny.

7 AMAZING ANIMALS

LEARNING OUTCOMES

I can ...

- understand texts about animals
- ask for and respond to information
- write an article
- understand how to use different past tense forms
- talk about and describe animals
- categorise vocabulary and identify word forms.

Start it!

1. What's happening in the big photo?
2. What do you know about this animal?
3. Guess three animals in the video. Watch and check.
4. How many animals can you remember from the video?

Watch video 7.1

p85

Language in action 7.2

p87

Language in action 7.3

p88

Everyday English 7.4

p90

Globetrotters 7.5

VOCABULARY
Animals

7.01 **1 Match ten animals with the photos. Listen, check, and repeat. Which four animals are not in the photos?**

bear	☐	crocodile	☐	donkey	☐
duck	☐	eagle	☐	giraffe	a
hippo	☐	horse	☐	lion	☐
monkey	☐	mouse	☐	parrot	☐
snake	☐	whale	☐		

1 ______ 2 ______ 3 ______ 4 ______

7.02 **2 Listen to the noises. Which animals do you hear from Exercise 1?**

1 ______ 3 ______ 5 ______
2 ______ 4 ______ 6 ______

3 Which of the animals have:

1 a tail? 2 feathers? 3 fur?

LEARN TO LEARN

Word categories

When you learn new words, put them into categories. This helps you remember the meaning.

4 Complete the categories with animals from Exercise 1. Add two more animals for each category.

Mammals	Birds	Reptiles
giraffe	*parrot*	*snake*

Use it!

5 Work with a partner. Guess the extra animals in each of your partner's categories.

6 Write new categories for the animals. Tell your partner the animals but NOT the categories! Can your partner guess your new categories?

Category 1: mouse, parrot, snake

Is your category 'pets'?

Explore it!

Guess the correct answer.

A blue whale's tongue weighs the same as …

a a crocodile. b an elephant. c a giraffe.

Find an interesting animal fact. Write a question for your partner to answer.

Animals with a Difference

Snowflake

From 1964 until 2003, there was a special gorilla in Barcelona Zoo. His name was Snowflake, and he was born in Africa. Snowflake was a celebrity in the zoo. He wasn't the same as the other gorillas because he was white. He was the world's only white gorilla.

Nómade

In the 1990s, in Mozambique, southern Africa, a baby elephant was born without tusks. Her name was Nómade. Her 11 sisters were born without them, too. In the 1930s, there weren't many African elephants without tusks, only 1%. But in some areas of Africa today, 98% of female elephants are born like this.

Artico

In 2004, a Bengal tiger called Artico was born in a wildlife centre in Alicante, Spain. But Artico wasn't like his parents. He was white with no stripes, but his parents weren't. They were orange with black stripes. Today, there are only about 20 Bengal tigers without stripes in the world.

GORILLA FACT FILE

WEIGHT	Up to 270 kg
HABITAT	African forests and mountains
FOOD	Fruit, leaves and plants
FACT	Gorillas are the largest mammals to build nests. They make a new nest every night.

AFRICAN ELEPHANT FACT FILE

WEIGHT	Up to 6,000 kg
HABITAT	African savannah and forests
FOOD	Grass, leaves, trees, fruit and plants
FACT	Elephants use their feet to listen.

BENGAL TIGER FACT FILE

WEIGHT	Up to 230 kg
HABITAT	Forests and mountains in South-East Asia
FOOD	Deer, buffalo, antelopes and other animals
FACT	There aren't two tigers with the same stripes.

READING

Fact files

1 Tell your partner two things you know about gorillas, elephants and tigers.

2 Look at the photos. What is different about Snowflake, Nómade and Artico?

7.03 **3** Read the text and the fact files. Check your answers to Exercise 2. Find out two things about each of the animals.

4 Read the sentences and write *R* (right), *W* (wrong) or *DS* (doesn't say).

1. Gorillas build nests. R
2. Elephants can hear with their feet. ____
3. Tigers are heavier than gorillas. ____
4. All tigers look different. ____
5. Only female elephants are born without tusks. ____
6. Gorillas are the heaviest animal. ____
7. There are more than 20 Bengal tigers without stripes. ____

5 Find words in the fact files for each of these categories. Think of two more words for each category.

Animals: gorilla ____________

Things animals eat: ____________

Habitats: ____________

Voice it!

6 Why do you think …

1. tigers have stripes?
2. gorillas build a nest every night?
3. some elephants are born without tusks?

Finished? p124 Ex 1

LANGUAGE IN ACTION

was/were, there was/were

Watch video 7.2
What colour was the flamingo when it was a baby?
What animals were there?

was/were	*there was/there were*
His name [1] was Snowflake.	**There** [2] ________ a special gorilla in the zoo.
They [3] ________ orange with black stripes.	**There were** lots elephants in the zoo.
Artico [4] ________ like his parents.	**There wasn't** another gorilla like him.
Were Artico's parents white? No, they [5] ________ .	**Were there** other white gorillas? No, **there weren't**.

1 **Complete the examples in the table above. Use the text on page 84 to help you.**

2 **Find information in the text to correct the sentences.**

1. Snowflake and Artico were black.
   They weren't black. They were white.
2. Snowflake was from Barcelona.
   He ________
3. Nómade was born in Spain.
   She ________
4. Nómade was an Indian elephant.
   She ________
5. Artico was a lion.
   He ________

3 **Complete the text with *was(n't)/were(n't)* or *there was(n't)/there were(n't)*.**

GIANT DRAGONS!

In the past, on the Island of Flores, [1] there were animals like elephants. But [2] ________ one difference: they [3] ________ very small. [4] ________ also Komodo dragons and huge rats on the island. [5] ________ people on Flores?
Yes, [6] ________ , but they [7] ________ very tall.
They [8] ________ only about one metre tall.
That's the size of a three-year-old! And their brain [9] ________ the size of an orange!

Use it!

4 **Write questions with *was/were*. Ask and answer with a partner.**

1. Where / born?
   Where were you born?
2. What / favourite subject at primary school?
3. What / favourite animal / when / you / six?
4. What / favourite film / when / you / seven?
5. Who / best friend / when / you / eight?
6. Where / you / at six o'clock on Sunday evening?
7. When / your last holiday?

Finished? p124 Ex 2

VOCABULARY AND LISTENING

Adjectives

7.04 **1 Circle words to describe photos 1–6. Listen, check and repeat. Can you guess the meaning of the other adjectives?**

2 Write opposite adjectives from Exercise 1 for the words below.

1 short ____long____
2 light ________
3 huge ________
4 quiet ________
5 safe ________

Use it!

3 Think of three animals. Write two sentences to describe each one. Tell your partner. Can they guess the animal?

It's quiet and fast. It sometimes lives in houses.

Is it a mouse?

A podcast

4 Discuss the questions with a partner.

1 What can parrots do?
2 Are parrots good pets? Why / Why not?

7.05 **5 Listen to the podcast and circle what it's about.**

a A hungry parrot
b An intelligent parrot
c A dangerous parrot

LEARN TO LEARN

Preparing to listen

Thinking about the questions before you listen can help you hear the correct answers.

6 Underline the question words in Exercise 7.

7.05 **7 Listen again and answer the questions.**

1 How old was Hannah? ________
2 Who was really noisy? ________
3 Who wasn't at home on the day of the story? ________
4 Why was Hannah's toast on the table? ________
5 Where was Meagan when Hannah ate the toast? ________

8 Work in pairs. Take turns to tell the story.

There was a parrot.

There was a little girl called Hannah.

Watch video 7.3
Which animals ran away?
Who touched a snake?

LANGUAGE IN ACTION

Past simple: regular and irregular verbs

Regular verbs	Irregular verbs	Past time expressions
They [1] lived in Denver.	Meagan **had** a pet parrot.	We heard the story **yesterday**.
They [2] ________ together at college.	Meagan **didn't** [3] ________ any children.	It **happened** more than ten years [4] ________ .

Irregular verbs p143 Pronunciation p142

1 **Complete the examples in the table above.**

2 **Complete the sentences. Correct three of the facts about the listening on page 86.**

Meagan …

1 didn't hear (not hear) Willie.
2 ________ (not make) Hannah toast.
3 ________ (leave) the toast on the table.
4 ________ (see) Hannah's face was blue.
5 and Willie ________ (not save) Hannah's life.

____
____
____

7.09 **3** **Complete the text. Listen and check.**

A Croc's Best Friend

Gilberto 'Chito' Shedden was a fisherman from Costa Rica. One day, he [1] saw (see) a crocodile in the river. It [2] ________ (have) an eye problem, so Chito [3] ________ (decide) to take the crocodile home. He [4] ________ (feed) the crocodile and [5] ________ (give) it medicine. He called it Pocho. Chito [6] ________ (not leave) Pocho, and at night they [7] ________ (sleep) in the same room. When Pocho was healthy again, Chito [8] ________ (take) him to the river. But Pocho [9] ________ (not want) to stay in the river, so he [10] ________ (follow) Chito home! Pocho and Chito [11] ________ (become) best friends until Pocho [12] ________ (die) a few years ago.

Use it!

4 **Write sentences with *ago*. Change the words in bold so that the sentences are true for you. Work with a partner and say your sentences. Are any the same?**

1 This lesson start / **thirty minutes**
This lesson started forty-five minutes ago.
2 I / get up / **four hours**
____
3 I / start / school / **seven years**
____
4 I / have / lunch / **an hour**
____
5 I / meet / my English teacher / **six months**
____

5 **Write three true and three false sentences about you. Use the past simple and past time expressions.**

6 **Take turns to say your sentences. Can your partner guess which are true and which are false?**

I went to Brazil on holiday last week.

False! You were at school last week.

Finished? p124 Ex 3

SPEAKING

Talk about a day out

7.10 **1 Listen to the conversation. Where was Martha yesterday?**

DANIEL	Hey, Martha. [1] How was the school trip yesterday?
MARTHA	[2] ____________ really cool! We went to a safari park.
DANIEL	Really? [3] ____________?
MARTHA	It was amazing!
DANIEL	Were there any elephants?
MARTHA	Yeah, there were, but I didn't see them.
DANIEL	I can't believe you didn't see any elephants. [4] ____________ lions?
MARTHA	Yeah, there was a family of lions. One of them looked inside our car.
DANIEL	Wow! No way!
MARTHA	Yup. It did. Then it climbed in the window and ate my lunch.
DANIEL	You're joking!
MARTHA	Of course I'm joking!

7.10 **2 Complete the conversation with the phrases from the *Useful language* box. Listen and check.**

Useful language

How was (the school trip)? It was (really cool).
What about(lions)? What was (it) like?

3 Look at the *Everyday English* box. Find and <u>underline</u> the phrases in the conversation.

Watch video 7.4 Everyday English

No way! Really?
Wow! You're joking!

4 Work with a partner. Practise the conversation.

PLAN

5 Work with a partner. Plan a conversation about a day out. Decide …

where you went. ____________

what you saw. ____________

what you didn't see. ____________

what happened. ____________

SPEAK

6 Practise the conversation with your partner. Remember to use verbs in the past and expressions from the *Useful Language* and *Everyday English* boxes.

CHECK

7 Work with another pair. Listen to their conversation and complete the notes.

Place: ____________

What they saw: ____________

What they didn't see: ____________

What happened: ____________

WRITING

An article

Skateboarding dog

By Lidia Watson

1 ☐ Can you skateboard? Tillman, a dog from California in the USA, could. He could skateboard 100 metres in 20 seconds!

2 ☐ In 2007, millions of people watched a video of him skateboarding. Soon, he became an international star. Tillman also liked other sports. He could snowboard and surf. Several years ago, he won first place in a surfing competition. On 27 October, 2015, Tillman died. He was 10 years old.

3 ☐ Now there are many skateboarding, snowboarding and surfing dogs. Some even have their own websites! Do you know any animals with amazing abilities?

1 **Look at the photo. Why do you think this dog is different? Read the article and check your ideas.**

2 **Match topics a–c with paragraphs 1–3.**

a Description of things Tillman did

b Introduction to the subject

c Conclusion that asks a question

3 **Read the article again and complete the notes.**

Skateboarding dog

Who Tillman

What ____________

Where ____________

4 **Look at the *Useful language* box. Find and underline the time expressions in the article.**

Useful language

In 2007 On 27 October, 2015 Several years ago

Get it right!

We use *on* for days and dates. *On Friday / On 27 October.*

We use *in* for months and years. *In October / In 2007.*

Write your own article about a famous animal.

PLAN

5 **Read the notes about a dog called Betsy. Use the notes to write an article or make your own notes about a famous animal.**

Most intelligent dog

Who Betsy

What understands more than 340 words

Where Vienna, Austria

Decide what information to include in each paragraph. Use the information in Exercises 2 and 3 to help you.

WRITE

6 **Write your article. Remember to include three paragraphs, the past simple and time expressions.**

CHECK

7 **Do you …**

- introduce the animal in the first paragraph?
- describe what the animal did?
- use time expressions?

Finished? p124 Ex 4

AROUND THE WORLD

READING
An article

7.11 **1** **Look at the photo. Where do you think the girl is from? Why is she special? Read the article to check your answers.**

2 **Read the article again and answer the questions.**

1. How old are boys when they learn to hunt with eagles? ________
2. How fast can eagles fly? ________
3. Where was Aisholpan's baby eagle when she found it? ________
4. Who was Aisholpan's trainer? ________
5. Who was the youngest person in the 2016 Golden Eagle Festival competition? ________

Globetrotters

Watch video 7.5
Four-legged Friends

- Where can you find camels?
- How much water can camels drink in ten minutes?
- What temperatures can camels survive in?

Voice it!

3 **Discuss the questions.**

1. Why do you think only boys usually hunt with eagles?
2. Why do you think Aisholpan won the competition?
3. Do you want to learn to hunt with eagles? Why / Why not?
4. Do you have any competitions like this in your country?

The Girl and the Golden Eagle

Can you imagine riding a horse in temperatures of –50 °C with a huge eagle on your arm?

The ancient tradition of eagle hunting started thousands of years ago in Mongolia. Traditionally, it was only for boys in Mongolia and this tradition continues today. Boys learn to hunt when they are only 13. They use eagles because they can fly up to 320 kph and can see animals from more than four kilometres away. There are about 400 male eagle hunters today. But no 13-year-old girls … until now.

The 2016 film, *The Eagle Huntress*, tells the story of Aisholpan. When she was young, Aisholpan took care of her father's eagle but she really wanted to be an eagle hunter like her father. So she went to the high Altai Mountains with her father to find a baby eagle to train. It wasn't easy. The climb to the eagle nest was difficult and dangerous. But Aisholpan did it. She found her baby eagle!

Aisholpan's father became her trainer. But was Aisholpan strong enough to hunt with the huge bird in freezing temperatures? Yes, because she was determined to succeed.

In 2016, Aisholpan competed in the Golden Eagle Festival. She was the first Mongolian girl to enter the competition. There were 70 competitors. She was the youngest and the only girl. And guess what? Her eagle won. What an amazing achievement!

LEARN TO LEARN

Noun and verb forms

When you learn a new word, try to learn some other forms of the word. This will help you to understand reading texts.

We can add different endings to verbs to make nouns, for example -*er*, -*ing*, -*or*, -*tion*, etc.

4 **Complete the table with words from the text.**

Verb	Noun (person)	Noun (thing)
1 *compete*	competitor	2 ______
hunt	3 ______	4 ______
train	5 ______	training
6 ______	climber	climbing
7 ______	learner	learning

5 **Write sentences with words from the table in Exercise 4. Take turns to say your sentences but do NOT say the word you chose. Can your partner guess your word?**

They (climb) a mountain every year.

Is the word 'climb'?

Explore it!

Guess the correct answer.

Eagle hunters use *male* / *female* eagles because they grow bigger and are more powerful.

Find three interesting facts about eagle hunters. Choose your favourite fact and write a question for your partner to answer.

OWN IT! The Culture Project Teacher's Resource Bank

7 REVIEW

VOCABULARY

1 Write the animals.

1 
monkey

2 
______

3 
______

4 
______

5 
______

6 
______

2 Complete the adjectives with the missing vowels.

1 w_i_ld
2 t__ny
3 n__ __sy
4 b__ __ __t__f__l
5 q__ __ __t
6 l__zy
7 d__ng__r__ __s
8 h__ __vy
9 c__t__
10 l__rg__
11 l__ng
12 cl__v__r

LANGUAGE IN ACTION

3 Joe and Sylvie went to a wildlife park last week. Write sentences with the correct form of *there was/were*.

1 Were there many animals? (?)
2 ______ two lions. (✓)
3 ______ an elephant with no tusks. (✗)
4 ______ a tiger with no stripes. (✓)
5 ______ a donkey. (✗)
6 ______ a white gorilla? (?)

4 Complete the text with the past simple of the verbs in brackets.

Mammoths [1] lived (live) many, many years ago in Asia, Europe and North America. They [2] ______ (die) because the weather [3] ______ (get) warmer and they [4] ______ (not can) find any food. They [5] ______ (be) about 3.5 m tall and [6] ______ (weigh) about 6,000 kg. Their tusks [7] ______ (be) very, very long – about five metres! They [8] ______ (be) herbivores, so they [9] ______ (not eat) other animals. They [10] ______ (eat) grass and plants and flowers.

Self-assessment

I can name fourteen animals in English.	☹	😐	☺
I can use adjectives to describe animals.	☹	😐	☺
I can use *was* and *were* to describe the past.	☹	😐	☺
I can use regular and irregular verbs to talk about the past.	☹	😐	☺

LEARN TO ... USE MIND MAPS

Mind maps can help you think of ideas and plan how to organise them.

1 Discuss the questions.

1 What is a mind map?
2 Why do people make mind maps?
3 Do you use mind maps?

2 Ahmet made a mind map to help him with a presentation. What is the topic?

____

3 Complete Ahmet's mind map with the words and phrases below.

1 football
2 Where?
3 magazines
4 at the weekend

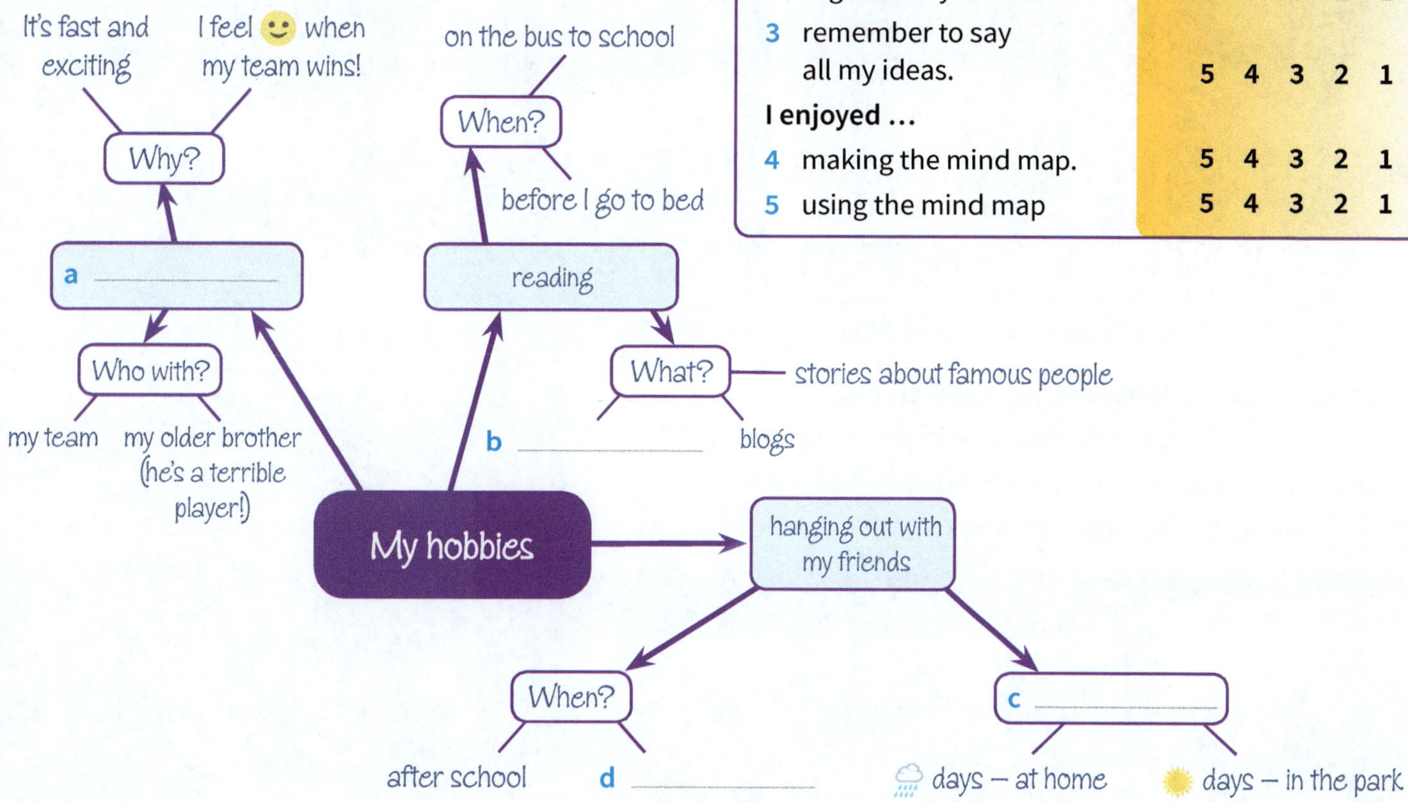

OWN IT!

4 Make a mind map about your favourite animal. Follow the instructions.

1 Write the topic in the middle.
2 Add three main ideas about the topic.
3 Write one or two questions about each main idea.
4 Write notes about your answers to each question.

5 Use your mind map to talk to your partner about your favourite animal.

6 Circle how you feel. Compare and discuss your answers with a partner.

The mind map helped me ...	**agree → disagree**
1 think of ideas.	5 4 3 2 1
2 organise my ideas.	5 4 3 2 1
3 remember to say all my ideas.	5 4 3 2 1
I enjoyed ...	
4 making the mind map.	5 4 3 2 1
5 using the mind map	5 4 3 2 1

8 LOST AND FOUND

LEARNING OUTCOMES

I can …

- understand texts about an unusual town and finding treasure
- help a friend
- write a blog post
- understand how to ask past simple questions
- talk about places in a city and personal possessions
- use compound nouns and photos to predict content
- do an interview.

Start it!

1 Describe the photo. Where do you think this is?

2 Before you watch, where do you look when you lose something?

3 What do archaeologists want to know? Watch and check.

4 What is your favourite treasure? Why?

Watch video 8.1

p97

Language in action 8.2

p99

Language in action 8.3

p100

Everyday English 8.4

VOCABULARY
Places in town

8.01 **1 Match the places in the box with the photos. Listen, check and repeat.**

aquarium	☐	bowling alley	a
car park	☐	cinema	☐
hospital	☐	ice rink	☐
post office	☐	shopping centre	☐
skate park	☐	sports centre	☐
swimming pool	☐		

2 Which places in Exercise 1 are in your town? Which ones do you sometimes or often go to? Compare with a partner.

LEARN TO LEARN

Compound nouns

There are lots of compound nouns in English. The two words together usually have a different meaning from the separate words.

3 Look at the places in Exercise 1. Which words are compound nouns? Can you think of any more compound nouns?

Use it!

4 Answer the questions. Write two more questions about the places in Exercise 1 for your partner to answer.

Where do you go to …

1 buy clothes and accessories? ______
2 see fish and sea creatures? ______
3 see a doctor? ______
4 watch a film? ______
5 do sports and exercise? ______
6 ______
7 ______

Explore it!

Guess the correct answer.

The Dubai Mall is one of the largest shopping centres in the world. There are 1,200 shops and there's also …

a an aquarium b a swimming pool c a skate park

Find another interesting fact about the Dubai Mall. Write a question for your partner to answer.

READING

An online travel article

Lost treasures

Last week, our travel writer, Marisa Castillo, visited the town of Villa Epecuén in Argentina and met its only inhabitant, Pablo Novak.

Pablo grew up in Villa Epecuén and until 1985 he had a normal family life there. On 10th November 1985, after weeks of heavy rain, a lake **flooded** the town and it gradually disappeared under 10 metres of water. All of the town's 1,500 **residents** left. In 2009, the water began to go down and Pablo decided to return.

Now he and his dogs live in an **abandoned** house with no electricity. One of his 21 grandchildren visits him every day and brings him food. He doesn't mind being the only person there. 'I am OK here. I am just alone. I read the newspaper. And I always think of the town's golden days,' Pablo said.

His **memories** of those golden days brought the town to life for me. As we walked past empty buildings, those places suddenly became family homes, noisy swimming pools, hotels full of **tourists** and busy car parks.

Comments

Libby: Did Pablo and the other residents move far away?

Marisa: No, they didn't. They moved to a town called Carhué about 7 km away.

Luca: 👍 Cool story! Did Pablo's wife want to go back to Villa Epecuén with him?

Marisa: No, she didn't. His wife and family started a new life in Carhué.

1 Look at the photo of the town. What do you think happened?

8.02 **2 Read the article and check your answers to Exercise 1.**

3 Find out what the words in bold in the article mean.

4 Read the article again and circle the correct answer.

1 Until 1985, Pablo lived … in Villa Epecuén.
   (a) with his family
   b on his own
   c with one of his grandchildren

2 When Villa Epecuén flooded, … of the residents stayed.
   a some b none c all

3 Pablo now lives … .
   a with his family
   b with a friend and his dogs
   c alone with his dogs

4 Pablo … being the only person in Villa Epecuén.
   a hates b loves c doesn't mind

5 Pablo spends time each day … .
   a reading the newspaper
   b shopping for food
   c sitting in the train station

6 Pablo has got … memories of the town in the past.
   a sad b happy c no

Voice it!

5 Discuss the questions.

1 Do you know any towns like Villa Epecuén?

2 Look at the questions in the Comments section. Think of two more questions to ask Marisa about Villa Epecuén.

Finished? p125 Ex 1

LANGUAGE IN ACTION

Past simple: questions

Watch video 8.2
What did he do at the weekend?
Did his parents like what he did?

	Yes/No questions		Short answers
Did	Pablo and the other residents	[1] *move* far away?	Yes, they **did**. / No, they [2] ________.
	Pablo's wife	[3] ________ to go back?	Yes, she **did**. / No, she [4] ________.

Pronunciation p142

1 **Complete the examples in the table above. Use the article on page 96 to help you.**

2 **Write past simple questions and answers. Check your answers in the article on page 96.**

1 the lake / flood / Villa Epecuén?
Did the lake flood Villa Epecuén? Yes, it did.

2 Villa Epecuén / disappear in 1985?
____

3 the residents / stay / after the flood?
____

4 the water / start / to disappear in 2009?
____

5 Pablo / return / in 2009?
____

8.05 **3** **Complete the conversation with the correct form of the verbs. Listen and check.**

ANNA [1] *Did* you *go* (go) to the ice rink last night?
CARLO Yes, I [2] ________.
ANNA [3] ________ you ________ (see) Jack there?
CARLO No, I [4] ________. I was with Tom and Kirsten.
ANNA [5] ________ you all ________ (have) a good time?
CARLO No, we [6] ________. It was freezing and the music was really bad.
ANNA Oh dear. [7] ________ you ________ (buy) some food later?
CARLO Yes, we [8] ________. We bought a pizza at the café.
ANNA [9] ________ you ________ (enjoy) it?
CARLO No, we [10] ________. It was disgusting!
ANNA Oh dear. Try the burger place next time.

Get it right!

Remember to use *did* and the infinitive in past simple questions.
Did Pablo return home? **NOT** ~~*Pablo returned home?*~~

8.06 **4** **Look at Simon's list. Write a conversation between Simon and his mum. Listen and check.**

do your homework ✓
cook dinner ✗
book the cinema tickets ✓
finish your science project ✗
phone grandpa ✓
tidy your bedroom ✗

Use it!

5 **Write past simple questions. Ask and answer with a partner.**

1 you / go / to the swimming pool last Saturday?
Did you go to the swimming pool last Saturday?

2 you and your family / watch TV last night?
____

3 you / have / a maths lesson yesterday?
____

4 your parents / drive / you to school today?
____

5 your best friend / text / you this morning?
____

Finished? p125 Ex 2

VOCABULARY AND LISTENING

Personal possessions

8.07 **1 Match the words in the box with the photos. Listen, check and repeat.**

bus pass	☐	camera	☐
concert ticket	1	headphones	☐
ID card	☐	keys	☐
laptop	☐	money	☐
passport	☐	phone	☐
portable charger	☐	tablet	☐

2 Look in your schoolbag. How many of the possessions in Exercise 1 have you got?

Use it!

3 Describe a possession you used yesterday. Can your partner guess?

I used this on the bus yesterday.

Your phone?

A radio interview

LEARN TO LEARN

Using photos to predict content

Before you listen, look carefully at any pictures. Think about the connection between them.

4 Look at the photos in Exercise 6 and read the sentences. Work with a partner and say what you think the story is about.

8.08 **5 Listen to the radio interview and check your answers to Exercise 4. Were you correct?**

8.08 **6 Listen again. Are the sentences *T* (true) or *F* (false)?**

1. Andres goes out every weekend to look for treasure. F
2. Andres uses special equipment when he does his hobby. ___
3. Detectorists always collect old drinks cans. ___
4. When detectorists find treasure, they dance. ___
5. Andres found some very old Roman money. ___

Voice it!

7 Discuss the questions.

1. Do you know anyone with an unusual hobby like Andres?
2. Imagine you find some ancient treasure. How do you feel? What do you do?

LANGUAGE IN ACTION
Past simple: *Wh*- questions

Watch video 8.3
What did Nick lose?
Where did Nick find them?

Where	did	you	go last weekend?
Who		you	go with?
What		your dad	do?
When		you	take that photo?
How		Andres	find the treasure?

1 **Look at the table above. Put the words in the correct order to write the questions. Match them with the answers.**

1 Andres / find / did / the treasure / when?
When did Andres find the treasure? [b]

2 did / Andres / find / where / the treasure? ______
______ [ ]

3 Andres / how / feel / did?
______ [ ]

4 he / what / did / do?
______ [ ]

5 send the photos to / did / Andres's dad / who? ______
______ [ ]

a Shocked.
b Last weekend.
c He shouted for his dad and did a dance.
d The local museum.
e In a field near his house.

8.09 **2** **Complete the conversations with the question words and the correct form of the verbs. Listen and check.**

A How much Where

A Hey. Cool headphones!
[1]Where did you get (get) them?
B I bought them online.
A [2]______ they ______ (cost)?
B €20.

B What Which Who

A [3]______ you ______ (do) on Saturday afternoon?
B I went to the cinema.
A [4]______ you ______ (go) with?
B I went with Lukas.
A [5]______ film ______ you ______ (see)?
B We saw the new Avengers film. It was amazing!

C When Where

A [6]______ your dad ______ (lose) his passport?
B He lost it yesterday.
A [7]______ he ______ (lose) it?
B I don't know but I know he needs to find it because we're going to Paris tomorrow!

3 **Have a conversation like conversation B in Exercise 2. Change the information so it is true for you.**

Use it!

4 **Think of your favourite possession. Write questions to guess your partner's possession. Ask and answer. Can you guess?**

1 when / get it? When did you get it?
2 why / want it? ______
3 where / buy it? ______
4 how much / cost? ______

When did you get it?

I got it for my 13th birthday.

Finished? p125 Ex 3

SPEAKING
Losing things

8.10 1 Listen to the conversation. Where is Billy's bus pass?

BILLY	I can't find my bus pass, Gemma.
GEMMA	Don't panic!
BILLY	I need it to get home.
GEMMA	Calm down. Let's think. [1] When did you last have it?
BILLY	On the bus this morning.
GEMMA	Right, OK. [2] ________________________.
BILLY	I can't remember.
GEMMA	Well, [3] ________________________.
BILLY	Yes, I did. I'm certain.
GEMMA	[4] ________________________?
BILLY	Maybe.
GEMMA	Right. What's that?
BILLY	Yesterday's lunch.
GEMMA	Gross! What's this?
BILLY	My bus pass. I don't know what to say.
GEMMA	Thanks, maybe?

8.10 2 Complete the conversation with the phrases from the *Useful language* box. Listen and check.

Useful language

Did you have it when you (got to school)?
Did you put it (in your bag)?
What did you do with it after that?
When did you last (have/use/see) it?

3 Look at the *Everyday English* box. Find and underline the phrases in the conversation.

WATCH VIDEO 8.4
Everyday English

Calm down. Don't panic!
Gross! Let's think.

4 Work with a partner. Practise the conversation.

PLAN

5 Work with a partner. Plan a conversation about losing something. Decide …

what you lost.

____

when you last had/used it.

____

where you were.

____

what you did with it.

____

SPEAK

6 Practise the conversation with your partner. Remember to use past simple questions and answers, the vocabulary from this unit and expressions from the *Useful language* and *Everyday English* boxes

CHECK

7 Work with another pair. Listen to their conversation and complete the notes.

What did they lose?

____

Did they find it? If so, where?

____

WRITING

A blog post

Tanya's *thoughts on life, the universe and the rest*

A bad day!

1 ☐ It started this morning. I didn't hear my alarm so I got up late. I didn't have time for breakfast and I couldn't find my bus pass so I ran all the way to school. It got worse!

2 ☐ My first class was maths – I forgot my book. Guess what? It didn't matter because we had a surprise test. It was really hard. 🙁

3 ☐ At lunchtime, I realised I didn't have any money so I didn't have any lunch. I went to the library instead. Bad news.

4 ☐ But the worst thing happened later. After school, I went to the skate park but I lost my mobile so I can't text, take any selfies or make calls. I'm using my brother's laptop to write this. Tragic. 😭

5 ☐ Did you all have a good Friday? What did you do? Let me know.

👍 *Friday, 26 June posted at 8.30 pm*

1 Read the blog post. Give one reason why Tanya had a bad day. ______________________

2 Read the blog post again. Put the events in Tanya's day in the correct order (1–5).

a ☐ She didn't have any lunch.
b [1] She didn't hear her alarm.
c ☐ She lost her mobile.
d ☐ She couldn't find her bus pass.
e ☐ She had a maths test.

3 Match topics a–e with paragraphs 1–5.

a ☐ In the morning
b [1] When it started
c ☐ The end of the day
d ☐ Sign off and ask two questions
e ☐ The middle of the day

Useful language

I didn't hear my alarm **so** I got up late.

4 Look at the *Useful language* box and underline more examples of *so* in the blog post.

5 Join the sentences using *so*.

1 I was late. I ran. I was late so I ran.
2 The students had a test. They revised.
____
3 We didn't have any money. We didn't buy any concert tickets. ______________________
____
4 Emma wanted to apologise. She rang me.
____

Write your own blog post about a bad day.

PLAN

6 Make notes about your bad day. Think about the answers to these questions.

When did the bad day start?
What problems did you have?
When did each problem happen?
What did you do?
How did you feel?

Decide what information to include in each paragraph. Use the information in Exercise 3 to help you.

WRITE

7 Write your blog post. Remember to include five paragraphs, the past simple for the questions at the end and the expression from the *Useful language* box.

CHECK

8 Do you …

- use a title for your blog post?
- use *so* to join ideas and explain the results?
- say how you felt on your bad day?

Finished? p125 Ex 4

THE HISTORY PROJECT

An interview

1 **Look at the photos. What's the connection between them?**

8.11 **2** **Listen to Ruby and Jacob's interview. Check your answers to Exercise 1. Were you correct?**

8.11 **3** **Listen again and answer the questions.**

1. How many people were there in Clarissa's family? Ten
2. What was her life like when she was younger? ______
3. What buildings were in Clarissa's street? ______
4. What happened to Cookie? ______
5. In Clarissa's opinion, what are the most important things in life? Do you agree? ______

8.12 **4** **Listen to a teacher talking about questions for a good interview. What are the three types of questions?**

5 **Look at the interview questions 1–6 on page 103. Are they open, closed or follow-up questions?**

6 **Read the *How to* box. Write the tips (a–h) in the table.**

Before the interview	During the interview	After the interview
______	a ______	______

How to do a recorded interview

a Keep the interview short.
b Use open and follow-up questions.
c Plan your questions.
d Introduce yourself.
e Record your interview on your phone.
f Send a thank you email / letter.
g Check you have everything you need.
h Say why you're doing the interview or why you want to interview the person.

7 **Do you think Ruby and Jacob followed all the tips?**

LIVING MEMORIES

Radley Boulevard 1947

Radley Boulevard today

Cookie

Clarissa 1949

Clarissa today

Interview questions for Clarissa Briggs

Date and time: 17th June, 10 am

Place: 937 Houston Street East

1 Where did you live as a child? open

2 What did you do each day? ______

3 Why did things change? ______

4 How did you feel about the change? ______

5 Who was Cookie? ______

6 What lessons for life did you learn from that experience? ______

PLAN

8 **Work in pairs. Choose a person to interview for the Living Memories project. Think about the things you want to know. Complete the steps below.**

Before the interview

- Plan and prepare your questions.

During the interview

- Introduce yourself.
- Record the interview or make notes.
- Listen carefully to the answers.

After the interview

- Thank the person.
- Type or write up the interview.
- Send the person a copy and a thank you email / letter.

PRESENT

9 **Play your recording to the class or display your written interviews on the wall with the photos. Remember to include polite language, photos of the person and place in the past and now, and follow the tips in *How to* do a recorded interview.**

CHECK

10 **Listen to or read your classmates' interviews and complete the notes.**

Who did they interview?

______

Which interview question was the most interesting?

______

Write down two interesting or surprising facts that you learned.

______

______

8 REVIEW

VOCABULARY

1 Match 1–6 with a–f to make places in a town.

1 bowling — a park
2 ice — b centre
3 post — c pool
4 shopping — d alley
5 skate — e office
6 swimming — f rink

2 Circle the correct words.

1 Laura always wears her *laptop / headphones* when she listens to music.
2 I can't get the bus home. I didn't bring my *passport / bus pass*.
3 My *phone / concert ticket* isn't working. I can't send any texts.
4 We want to buy some sandwiches. Have you got any *keys / money*?
5 They're great photos. Did you use your new *camera / charger*?

LANGUAGE IN ACTION

3 Write the past simple questions 1–5 and match them with the answers a–e.

1 you / have / an egg for breakfast this morning?
______ ☐
2 you and Mike / go / shopping yesterday?
______ ☐
3 Teresa / send / you a text this morning?
______ ☐
4 your new passport / arrive / last week?
______ ☐
5 your parents / watch / the concert?
______ ☐

a No, but she rang me last night.
b Yes, it did.
c No, I always have toast.
d No, they didn't.
e Yes, we bought some clothes at the market.

4 Look at the answers and write the questions. Use the question words in the box.

How many	What	When	Where	Who

1 A you / on TV last night?
______
B We watched a really exciting film.
2 A your cousin / her keys?
______
B She lost them at the shopping centre.
3 A Ana's grandparents / to Spain?
______
B They came here in 1997.
4 A Martin / at the cinema?
______
B He met Jamie and Emma.
5 A eggs / you?
______
B I bought twelve.

Self-assessment

I can name eleven places in a town in English.
I can name twelve personal possessions in English.
I can ask *Yes/No* questions using the past simple.
I can ask *Wh-* questions using the past simple.

LEARN TO LEARN

LEARN TO … IMPROVE YOUR WRITING

When you write something, ask your partner to check it. This improves your writing and your partner's writing.

1 **Read the writing task and Oleg's story. Correct Oleg's mistakes to help him improve.**

WRITING TASK

Write a story about a fun day you had in your town.

- Write between 50 and 70 words.
- Use words for places in town and personal possessions.
- Use the past simple.
- Describe people, places and things to make it interesting.
- Give your story a title.

Don't forget to use punctuation and check your spelling!

A nice day I had in town by Oleg

Last Saturday it [1]is __was__ my birthday. My [2]parent ________ gave me a skateboard. In the morning I went to the skate [3]parc ________ to try it. In the afternoon, I met my friend Boris. We love fish, so we visited the aquarium and saw lots of fish. I didn't [4]took ________ any photos because I [5]leaved ________ my phone at home, but Boris took lots. In the evening I [6]have ________ dinner with my family in a restaurant.

2 **Circle the emojis in the checklist about Oleg's writing.**

Checklist for story writing task

Did he/she …	Oleg			My partner		
1 write about the topic?	🙁	😐	🙂	🙁	😐	🙂
2 write between 50 and 70 words?	🙁	😐	🙂	🙁	😐	🙂
3 use words for places in town?	🙁	😐	🙂	🙁	😐	🙂
4 use words for possessions?	🙁	😐	🙂	🙁	😐	🙂
5 use the past simple?	🙁	😐	🙂	🙁	😐	🙂
6 make it interesting?	🙁	😐	🙂	🙁	😐	🙂
7 add a title?	🙁	😐	🙂	🙁	😐	🙂
8 use punctuation?	🙁	😐	🙂	🙁	😐	🙂
9 use correct spelling?	🙁	😐	🙂	🙁	😐	🙂

3 **Work in pairs. Imagine your partner is Oleg. Use your answers in the checklist in Exercise 2 to tell him what you like and what he can improve.**

You used words for places in a town. That was good!

Thanks!

You can improve your past simple. You made some mistakes.

OK. Thank you for your help.

OWN IT!

4 **Write your own story for the task in Exercise 1.**

5 **Give your partner your story. Circle the emojis in the checklist in Exercise 2 about your partner's story.**

6 **Use your answers in the checklist to tell your partner what you like and what they can improve.**

9 SUMMER FUN

LEARNING OUTCOMES

I can ...

- understand texts about an adventure weekend and holidays
- make suggestions and respond to them
- write an email
- understand how to use the future tenses
- talk about outdoor life and holidays
- make collocations and spidergrams and understand different types of English.

Start it!

1 Look at the photo. Do you try new sports or activities when you are on holiday? What did you try?

2 Before you watch, what do people do on holiday?

3 Where did Juno and Raúl go on holiday? Watch and check.

4 Which holiday do you prefer? Juno or Raúl's? Why?

Watch video 9.1

p109

Language in action 9.2

p111

Language in action 9.3

p112

Everyday English 9.4

p114

Globetrotters 9.5

VOCABULARY
Outdoor life

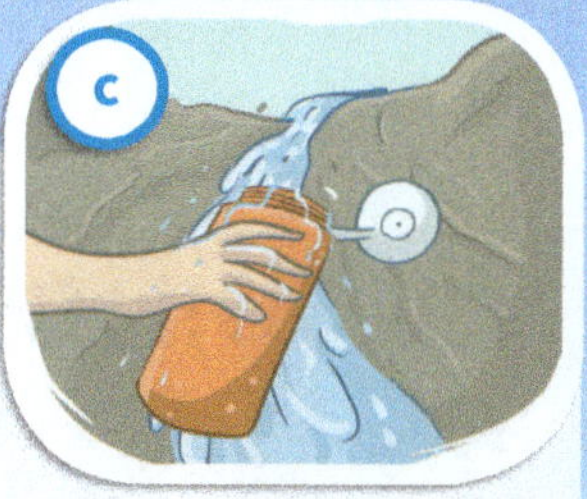

9.01 **1 Match the activities in the box with the pictures. Listen, check and repeat.**

build a shelter	☐	identify plants	☐
catch fish	☐	light a fire	☐
collect wood	☐	pick fruit	a
cook over a campfire	☐	read a map	☐
find food and water	☐	use a compass	☐

9.02 **2 Circle the correct expressions. Listen and check.**

1 A I'm thirsty.
  B OK. *Let's find some water* / *light a fire*.
2 A I'm hungry.
  B Why don't we *build a shelter* / *pick some fruit to eat*?
3 A This plant looks delicious. Let's try it.
  B No. It's important to *collect wood* / *identify plants* before you eat them.
4 A Oh no! We're lost. Can you *read a map* / *identify plants*?
  B Of course, but we don't know where we are. Let's *cook over a campfire* / *use a compass* first.

LEARN TO LEARN

Collocation

Some verbs and nouns go together in English. Try to learn verbs in a phrase with a noun.

3 Look at the activities in Exercise 1 again. Take turns to say a noun or a verb for your partner to complete the phrase. How many can you remember?

4 Complete the table with another noun that goes with each verb in Exercise 1.

Verb	Noun	Verb	Noun
build	a house	identify	
catch		light	
collect		pick	
cook		read	
find		use	

Use it!

5 Discuss the questions.

1 Which activities in Exercise 1 can you do?
2 Which ones do you think are the most useful? Why?
3 Which ones do you want to learn?

Explore it!

Guess the correct answer.

Mauro Prosperi ran a marathon in the Sahara Desert in 1994 but he got lost. How long did he survive without water?

a one day b ten days c three weeks

Find an interesting fact about people's amazing survival skills. Write a question for your partner to answer.

READING
A leaflet

1 **Look at the photos. What do you think the leaflet is about? What do you want to know about it?**

9.03 2 **Match the questions (a–d) with the right places in the leaflet (1–4). Read and check your answers.**

a What will you eat?
b Who will look after you?
c Where will you sleep?
d What will you do during the weekend?

3 **Guess the meaning of the words in bold in the leaflet.**

4 **Choose the correct answer. Which person …**

You Adem Havva

1 will practise their wood skills? You
2 will learn new things? ______
3 will organise a cooking competition? ______
4 will build a shelter? ______
5 knows about wild food? ______
6 knows how to track animals? ______

Voice it!

5 **Discuss the questions.**

1 What do you think is the most interesting part of Wild Weekend?
2 Why is it important …
to be careful when lighting a fire?
to identify plants before eating them?

Finished? p126 Ex 1

WILD WEEKEND

Do you want a new adventure this summer?
Join us at one of our WILD centres in Turkey.
Every weekend from Friday to Sunday.

1 ☐
In a bed? In a tent? No, you'll sleep in a shelter. You'll build it yourself with **leaves** and **branches**.

2 ☐
You won't be near any shops or a supermarket so you'll find your own food. You'll learn to catch fish, collect fruit and identify plants to eat.

3 ☐
DAYTIMES
Why not try some of our amazing adventure activities?
- Go sea kayaking or diving in the sea.
- Go for a bike ride or go horse riding in the mountains.
- Learn to track animals or practise your wood skills.

EVENINGS
- Get to know your new friends and compare your WILD days.
- Sing, listen to ancient Turkish legends, cook potatoes over the campfire and relax.

4 ☐
MEET YOUR INSTRUCTORS!

Hi! I'm Adem. I'm an **expert** in extreme survival. I'll teach you survival skills for life. You'll also learn how to **track** animals and how to work with wood. You'll learn new things about yourself and you'll begin to love outdoor life.

Hi! I'm Havva and I'll help you to find, prepare and cook your own food. You won't want to eat food from a supermarket ever again! Look out for my campfire cooking challenge! Will you be a winner?

Join us for a WILD WEEKEND! You'll learn new skills, make new friends for life and have fun! Will you want to do it again? Of course, you will! For more information and booking details, visit our website now!

LANGUAGE IN ACTION
Future with *will/won't*

Watch video 9.2
Where will he sleep? What will they do there?

I/you/he/she/it/we/they
I'**ll teach** you survival skills.
You [1] 'll ______ sleep in a shelter.
You [2] ______ ______ near any shops.
[3] ______ you ______ a winner?
Yes, you **will**. / No, you **won't**.
What [4] ______ you **eat**?

1 **Complete the examples in the table above. Use the leaflet on page 108 to help you.**

2 **Complete the summary with *will* or *won't*. Check your answers in the leaflet on page 108.**

Wild Weekend

What [1] will you do?
You [2] ______ sleep in your own bed.
You [3] ______ build a shelter and sleep outdoors.
You [4] ______ buy your food in shops or supermarkets.
You [5] ______ find and cook your own food.
You [6] ______ learn new skills for life.
[7] ______ you have fun? Yes, you [8] ______.

3 9.04 **Complete the TV advert with the correct form of *will* and the verbs in the box. Listen and check.**

choose	get	not have	not see	~~spend~~	survive	work

TEEN CHALLENGE!

A group of five young teenagers [1] will spend three nights alone on an island.

In tonight's programme the group [2] ______ important information about the challenge and they [3] ______ five items to take with them.

For three nights, these young teenagers:

- [4] ______ their family or friends.
- [5] ______ phones or laptops.
- [6] ______ together to find shelter, food and water.

[7] ______ they ______ the toughest three days of their lives?

Watch tonight and find out!

Use it!

4 **You will interview one of the people in *Teen Challenge*. Write questions to ask about how they will survive on the island. Use the ideas below or your own ideas.**

1 miss your family and friends?
Will you miss your family and friends?
2 survive without your mobile?
______
3 learn new skills?
______
4 sleep in a tent?
______
5 have fun?
______

5 **Work with a partner. Ask and answer.**

Will you miss your family and friends?

Yes, I will.

Finished? p126 Ex 2

VOCABULARY AND LISTENING

Holidays

9.05 **1 Match the words with the photos. Listen, check and repeat.**

apartment	☐	B&B (bed & breakfast)	☐		
camper van	☐	caravan	☐	chalet	☐
cottage	☐	hotel	☐	tent	☐
youth hostel	1				

2 Which two types of accommodation do you think are best for each of these holidays?

1 a cheap beach holiday ______

2 a skiing holiday ______

3 a comfortable city holiday ______

4 a driving tour across the country ______

LEARN TO LEARN

Personalising spidergrams

Personalising a spidergram with colours or pictures can help you remember vocabulary more easily.

3 Make a spidergram with words from Exercises 1 and 2 in your notebook. How many more words can you add?

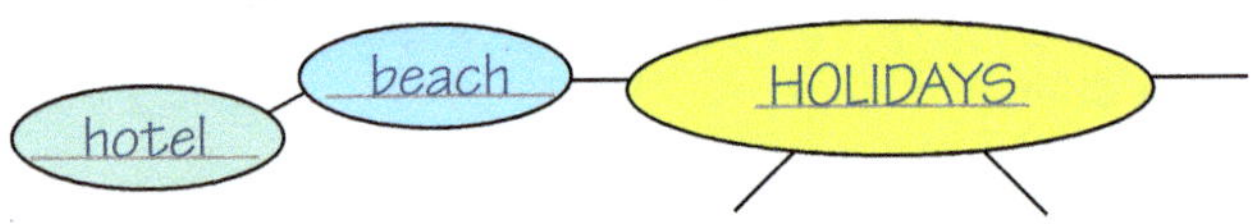

Use it!

4 Write sentences about your ideal type of holiday and place to stay. Compare with a partner.

1 summer or winter holiday

2 adventure holiday or weekend break

My ideal winter holiday is a skiing holiday and I want to stay in a chalet.

A conversation

9.06 **5 Listen. What are Matteo and Libby talking about?**

9.06 **6 Listen again. Write *M* (Matteo) or *L* (Libby).**

Who …

1 doesn't want to stay in a village? ___

2 has got a younger brother and sister? ___

3 talks about the tallest building in the world? ___

4 can ski on holiday? ___

9.06 **7 Complete the table with the correct information. Listen again and check.**

	Matteo and his parents	Libby and her parents
1 Accommodation	camper van	______
2 Start of holiday trip	______	______
3 Length of holiday trip	______	______
4 Destination(s)	______	______

Voice it!

8 Discuss the questions.

1 What is your dream holiday?

2 What types of holiday and holiday accommodation are popular in your country?

LANGUAGE IN ACTION
Present continuous for future

Watch video 9.3
Where is the school band going?
How long are they staying there?

Present continuous: to talk about fixed arrangements in the future
I'm going to a football camp for two weeks in June.
They**'re working** in July.
She **isn't staying** in a chalet.
Are they **working** in July? Yes, they [1] ________. / No, **they** [2] ________.
Where [3] ________ you **staying**? What [4] ________ she **doing** in July?

1 **Complete the examples in the table above.**

2 **Write questions with the present continuous. Match them with the correct answers.**

1 where / Matteo / spend / July?
Where is Matteo spending July? [e]

2 what / Matteo's parents / do / on 1st August?
________ [ ]

3 Matteo / travel / on his own?
________ [ ]

4 where / Libby / go / on holiday?
________ [ ]

5 when / she / leave?
________ [ ]

a No, he isn't. He's travelling with his family.
b She's going to Dubai.
c She's leaving on 29th July.
d They're hiring a camper van.
e He's spending it in his grandma's village.

be going to

***be going to*: to talk about future intentions**
We[1]'re **going to visit** a water park.
Matteo **isn't** [2] ________ **to travel** in France.
Are you **going** [3] ________ **go** on holiday this summer?

Pronunciation p142

3 **Complete the examples in the table above.**

4 **Write questions with *be going to*. Write the answers.**

1 Matteo and Libby / stay at home / this summer?
Are Matteo and Libby going to stay at home this summer? No they aren't.

2 who / swim / in six different swimming pools?
____
____

3 Libby / go up / the tallest building in the world?
____
____

4 what / Matteo / do / in each city?
____
____

Use it!

5 **Write questions and answers with *be going to* to talk about your intentions this summer.**

1 learn to make pizza (✓)
Are you going to learn to make pizza? Yes, I am.

2 sleep in a tent (✗)
____

6 **Write one arrangement and one intention you have for this summer. Ask and answer with a partner.**

1 ________
2 ________

What are you going to do this summer?

I'm going on holiday in August.

What are you going to do on holiday?

I'm going to visit lots of museums.

Finished? p126 Ex 3

SPEAKING

Making suggestions and responding

EMRE We're having the end-of-term event next Saturday.
NADIA Great! [1] *What are we going to do?*
EMRE That's why you're both here. Ideas, please!
NADIA I'm on it. [2] ________________?
EMRE [3] ________________. It's complicated and we'll never agree on a film.
AYA OK. Forget that. [4] ________________?
EMRE According to my weather app, it will rain. [5] ________________.
AYA We can have a danceathon indoors or outdoors. Easy!
EMRE OK. [6] ________________! What are you doing on the 26th, Nadia?
NADIA I'm going on holiday. I won't be here.
EMRE Nadia! You're unbelievable!
AYA Don't worry. You can count on me!

9.09 **1** **Listen to the conversation. What do they decide to do?**

9.09 **2** **Complete the conversation with the phrases from the *Useful language* box. Listen and check.**

Useful language

What about a (film night)?	I'm not sure about that.
What are we going to do?	I'd rather not do that.
Why don't we (have a picnic)?	Let's do that!

Get it right!

We say: *I'm going on holiday.* **NOT** ~~*I'm going on holidays.*~~

3 **Look at the *Everyday English* box. Find and <u>underline</u> the phrases in the conversation.**

Watch video 9.4
Everyday English

Easy! Forget that. I'm on it!
You're unbelievable!

4 **Work with a partner. Practise the conversation.**

PLAN

5 **Work with a partner. You are organising an end-of-term event. Ask for suggestions and respond. Use the ideas below or your own ideas.**

a visit to a theme park · a barbecue · a beach sports day · a fancy-dress party

SPEAK

6 **Practise the conversation with your partner. Remember to use *will*, *be going to* and the present continuous, the vocabulary from this unit and expressions from the *Useful language* and *Everyday English* boxes.**

CHECK

7 **Work with another pair. Listen to their conversation and complete the notes.**

Which end-of-term ideas did they talk about? ________________

____

What event do they decide on?

____

What event do you want to go to?

____

WRITING
An email

Hi Javi,

1 ☐ It was great to hear from you. I'm really excited about next week, too. I think you'll love England and Wales. It's a bit different from Spain.

2 ☐ Here are the arrangements. We're spending the weekend at home in Chester. We're going to sleep in a tent in the garden. It won't rain. It never rains in August! Honest!

3 ☐ On Monday, we're going to leave early in the morning to drive to the beach. We're staying in a cottage in Wales for three days. I think it looks amazing. I'm going to go swimming every day but the water will probably be very cold! My dad is going to teach us to catch fish and then we can cook them!

4 ☐ It'll be great to meet you in person. I'm going to meet you at the airport with my parents. Our car is quite small. Are you going to bring a big bag? It will be a busy week but it will be fun! See you on 1st August!

Martin

1 **Read the email quickly. Why is Martin writing to Javi?**

2 **Match topics a–d with paragraphs 1–4.**

- a End the email
- b Respond to your penfriend's last email
- c Describe the week ahead
- d Describe the weekend

3 **Complete the *Useful language* box with *at*, *in* or *on*. Use Martin's email to help you.**

Useful language

1 in the morning	4 ____ August
2 ____ Monday	5 ____ 1st August
3 ____ home	6 ____ the airport

Write an email to a penfriend.

PLAN

4 **Your penfriend is coming to stay for a week. Make notes about these things for your email.**

your arrangements

____

things you intend to do

____

predictions about what will happen

____

the place you are meeting them

____

Decide what information to include in each paragraph. Use the information in Exercise 2 to help you.

WRITE

5 **Write your email. Remember to include four paragraphs, *will*, *be going to* and the present continuous for future, and expressions from the Useful language box.**

CHECK

6 **Do you …**

- include an arrangement and a prediction for the weekend and the week ahead?
- make predictions about what will or won't happen?
- tell your penfriend where you are going to meet them?

Finished? p126 Ex 4

AROUND THE WORLD

READING
A webpage

1 Circle the answer you think is correct.

1. More than *9* / *11* million American children and teenagers are going to a summer camp this year.
2. The first American summer camp opened more than *50* / *150* years ago.

9.10 **2 Read the webpage and check your answers to Exercise 1. Write two more things you would like to know about American summer camps.**

____

____

3 Read the webpage again. Match the sentences with the camps 1–4.

a You will work with professional coaches. 3
b It lasts for three weeks. ___
c You will spend a month on this camp. ___
d This camp lasts for two weeks. ___
e You won't hear any English while you are on this camp. ___
f You can only do this course if you are not a beginner.

Globetrotters
Watch video 9.5
A summer camp in ...

- How long is the camp in Costa Rica?
- Which animal will you protect?
- What skills will you learn?

4 Write the adjectives for nouns 1–6.

1. beauty beautiful
2. music ______
3. nature ______
4. profession ______
5. success ______
6. wonder ______

Voice it!

5 Discuss the questions.

1. Do you think summer camps make you a more independent person?
2. Do you think it is important to be independent? Why?

Your Guide to American Summer Camps

What are you going to do in the summer vacation? Here in the USA, more than 11 million children and teenagers are going to summer camps. The first summer camp opened more than 150 years ago and there are now more than 1,200 summer camps to choose from.

Here are our four favorite camps this week.

1 Tech Camp, Massachusetts

You'll be in a great university in the state, at the heart of technology! In just three weeks, you'll learn to build robots with our older students. They'll help you to develop useful skills like game and web design. You'll stay in an apartment on our beautiful campus and experience college life.

LEARN TO LEARN

Understanding different types of English

Different English-speaking countries use different words and expressions. Make a note of them in your notebook.

6 **Is the webpage in American English or British English?**

7 **Look at the highlighted words in the webpage. Match them with the British English words.**

1 centre *center*
2 football ______
3 favourite ______
4 holiday ______
5 flat ______
6 theatre ______

9.11 **8** **Match the British English words with the American English words. Listen and check.**

British English	American English
autumn	candy
chips	eraser
garden	fall
rubber	fries
rubbish	garbage
sweets	pants
trousers	yard

Explore it!

Is the sentence true or false?

In the state of Georgia, it's illegal to live on a boat for more than 30 days. ___

Find out another interesting or unusual law about an American state and write a question for your partner to answer.

OWN IT! The Culture Project Teacher's Resource Bank

Search camps > | Age | State | Length   Find a camp now

2 Languages for Life, Georgia

Learn a new language! Choose from Arabic, Chinese and lots more! You'll live and sleep in the language and culture. You won't speak English for a month! In your free time, why not visit the world's largest aquarium or one of Georgia's wonderful museums?

3 Advanced Soccer Skills, California

Los Angeles has a long history of sport – the Summer Olympics in 1932 and 1984 and in 2028 the Olympics will be here again! In just one week, our professional coaches will use your natural talent to teach you amazing new soccer skills. Sorry no beginners!

4 Theater School, New Jersey

New Jersey is home to one of the most successful performing arts centers in the USA. Develop your musical talents or choose from circus skills, magic, public speaking or acting! After two weeks here, you'll perform live on the last day.

9 REVIEW

VOCABULARY

1 Match the verbs with the nouns.

1	use	a	a map
2	identify	b	a shelter
3	build	c	fish
4	catch	d	plants
5	read	e	a compass

2 Write the words for holiday accommodation.

1 This is part of a larger building. You have your own bedroom, kitchen and bathroom.
____

2 This is a cheap and simple type of shelter. You don't sleep in a bed. ______________

3 You share a room with other people in this place.
____

4 You travel and sleep in this and you don't need a car. ______________

LANGUAGE IN ACTION

3 Complete the sentences with *will/won't* and a verb from the box.

have speak win

1 I know you ______________ an amazing holiday in Turkey.

2 She ______________ any English in Russia.

3 ________ your country ________ the next World Cup?

4 Complete the conversation with the present continuous form of the verbs.

DAN Hi, Gabi. What [1] ________ you ________ (do) on Saturday?

GABI I [2] ______________ (meet) Louisa in town. Why?

DAN Matt and Clara [3] ______________ (come) to my house to organise a surprise party for Gino.

GABI Really? When [4] ________ you ________ (have) the party?

DAN On 15th September. Can you come?

GABI I think so. I [5] ______________ (not do) anything that weekend.

DAN Great!

5 Write sentences with the correct form of *be going to*.

1 ________ they ______________ to a summer camp this year? (go)

2 I ______________ early on Saturday! (not get up)

3 Becca ______________ all the food for the party. (cook)

4 We ______________ in a caravan this summer. (not stay)

6 Circle the correct verbs.

1 *I'm going to visit / I'll visit* my cousins in Paris in May.

2 Which subjects *are you choosing / will you choose* next year?

3 Jack can't come to the cinema tomorrow. *He's working / He'll work.*

4 *Will Kate want / Is Kate wanting* to come to the cinema with us tomorrow?

Self-assessment

I can name ten outdoor life activities in English.

I can talk about places to stay on holiday.

I can use *will* and *won't* to talk about the future.

I can use the present continuous to talk about arrangements and *be going to* to talk about intentions in the future.

LEARN TO ... MAKE AN ACTION PLAN

An action plan can help you improve a little every day.

1 **Read the texts and write *S* (Sasha) or *E* (Elif).**

Who ...

1 watches films? S
2 reads blogs? ___
3 watches online videos? ___
4 reads books? ___
5 listens to songs? ___
6 chats with a friend? ___
7 uses an app? ___

I have an app on my phone with flashcards. I use it a lot and sometimes I watch films in English. I also love English pop music. I find the words of songs online, check their meaning, and sing in my bedroom!

I read fashion blogs in English, and lots of books too. Also, my best friend Anita and I sometimes chat in English. I don't usually watch films, because they're difficult, but I watch lots of videos online.

2 **Choose three ways to practise English from Exercise 1. Tell your partner why you want to try them.**

I chose 'read a blog'.

Me, too! Why did you choose that?

Because I love reading online.

3 **Write the three things you chose in Exercise 2 and how often you will do them.**

read a blog : twice a week
1 ___ : ___
2 ___ : ___
3 ___ : ___

OWN IT!

4 **Use your answers to Exercise 3 to make an action plan.**

Action plan							
	Monday	Tuesday	Wednesday	Thursday	Friday	Saturday	Sunday
read a blog	✓			✓			
1 ___							
2 ___							
3 ___							

5 **Tell your partner about your action plan. Are there any things you can do together?**

What are you going to do?

I'm going to watch a film in English once a week.

We can do that together! You can come to my house.

5 FINISHED?

1 Use the code to complete the sentences about Dean's look.

A	C	D	E	F	G	H	I	J	K	L	M	N	O
✦	☐	○	✪	✓	💧	◗	🔔	∞	■	☺	✵	☼	⌘
P	**R**	**S**	**T**	**U**	**V**	**W**							
✈	♥	❖	●	◆	⇧	◎							

Dean likes playing sport so he wears ●♥✦🔔☼✪♥❖ [1] trainers , ∞⌘💧💧✪♥❖ [2] ________ and ●-❖◗🔔♥●❖ [3] ________. At school he wears a ◆☼🔔✓⌘♥✵ [4] ________ and a ☐✦✈ [5] ________.

2 Match photos a–c with sentences 1–3.

a

b

c

1 Ingrid is eating an apple and checking her phone. She's wearing a jacket and jeans.
2 Holly is sitting and eating an apple. She's wearing a black jacket.
3 Maria is walking and smiling. She's wearing a jacket and a dress.

3 Complete the words. Use the letters in circles to find the secret word.

Ignacio is a fashion photographer. He takes photos of models for magazines. Today he is [1]t a (k) i n g photos of his friend, Naomi. Ignacio often [2]c_ ( ) _ _ here to work with Naomi. She's [3]w_ ( ) _ _ _ _ a grey dress and a black hat. She always [4]w( ) _ _ _ a lot of accessories. Naomi loves clothes and fashion. She [5]s_ _ _ _ _ ( ) fashion design at college and she [6]_ _ _ _ _ her own clothes.

Secret word: ________

4 Read the clues and write the accessories.

1 You put me on your hands in cold weather. gloves
2 I go on your eyes in the summer. ________
3 You keep your money here. ________
4 You use me in the rain. ________
5 You wear me on your arm. I tell you the time. ________
6 I keep your neck warm. ________

6 FINISHED?

1 Find five sports words in the box. The letters for each words are in the same colour. Put the letters in order and write the words under the correct verb.

R	E	B	M	B	Y	Y	I
C	A	I	G	H	T	K	S
L	U	O	E	N	G	C	A
C	T	L	H	O	I	G	Y

play	go	do
h________	c________	a________
r________		y________

2 Follow the lines to find the comparisons. Write the sentences.

A basketball	more popular	gymnastics
Windsurfing	bigger	a basketball
A football	slower	a tennis ball
Football	smaller	rugby
Yoga	more difficult	sailing

1 A basketball is bigger than a tennis ball.
2 ____________________
3 ____________________
4 ____________________
5 ____________________

3 Use the table to write the adjectives. Complete the questions a–e with the superlative forms of the correct adjectives. Answer them for you.

1	2	3	4	5	6	7	8	9	10	11	12	13
A	B	C	D	E	F	G	H	I	J	K	L	M
N	O	P	Q	R	S	T	U	V	W	X	Y	Z

1

7	1	6	7	12
T	A	S	T	Y

2

8	1	3	3	12

3

7	1	12	12

4

9	1	7	5	5	5	6	7	9	1	7

5

5	11	3	5	1	6	9	9	5

a What is __________ thing you own?
b Who is __________ person in your class?
c What is __________ food you eat?
c Who is __________ person in your family?
d What is __________ book you know?

4 Use the picture to complete the crossword with sports verbs.

Across
1 Oscar
4 Kyle
5 Melissa

Down
1 Katya and Simon
2 Jimena
3 Dylan

7 FINISHED?

1 Read the clues and put the letters in the correct order to make words. Write the answers.

1 This reptile has no arms or legs.
NAKES snake

2 This mammal lives in the sea.
HELAW ______

3 Some people are scared of this very small animal.
SEMOU ______

4 This bird is the national symbol of the US.
GALEE ______

5 This animal has a trunk and usually has two tusks.
THAPELEN ______

2 Sarah went to a safari park. Look closely at her photos and write the animals that were there.

1 There was a gorilla.
2 There were elephants and a giraffe.
3 ______
4 ______
5 ______

3 Complete the crossword with the past simple of the verbs.

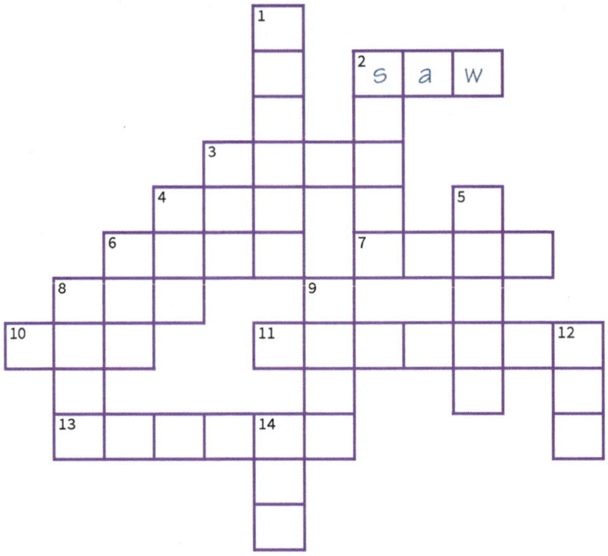

Across
2 see
3 give
6 make
7 take
10 feed
11 learn
13 teach

Down
1 become
2 sleep
4 be
5 find
8 leave
9 go
12 do
14 have

4 Which animal is it? Read the sentences and tick the correct photo.

This is a wild animal. It is large and heavy. Most people think it isn't cute and it is very dangerous. It lives on land and in the water.

8 FINISHED?

1 **Write the places 1–5 in the crossword. Put the letters in the blue column in the correct order to make a word. Write the mystery word.**

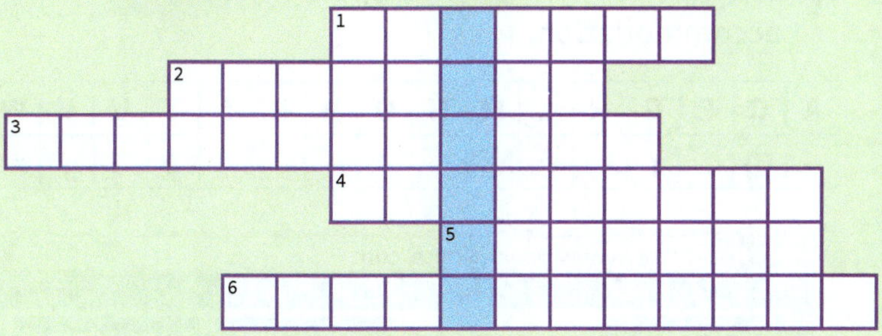

Mystery word: ________

2 **Circle the words to make questions.**

1 buygulpdodidhuilgeyoursdadjklfoundgefindkolhisqwalletotr?

2 lkifydidaywshechaveklpohadsanydtypizza?

3 miumdidqeidonhyoubvisitklwivbghyourmklawdgrandma?

4 safdidalkshyiheyatgomwenttoasthekfgicexprinkrew?

5 erkldideljoktheytifgofemshoppingoreltogetheriful?

3 **Write the words in the correct order to make questions. Match the questions to the photos a–e.**

1 did / where / she / that / buy / dress?
Where did she buy that dress?

2 you / see / at / pool? / the / did / who
____

3 you / the / do / at / did / what / weekend?
____

4 when / you / did / your / bike? / get
____

5 box? / open / how / did / you / the
____

4 **Look at the pictures and complete the sentences.**

1 Ellie didn't have much  *money* so she couldn't buy a  ________.

2 When my  ________ stopped working I used my  ________.

3 You can use your  ________ or your  ________ to show who you are.

4 Sam lost his  ________ and his  ________ on his way to school.

9 FINISHED?

1 Circle ten words. Write the collocations to make five outdoor activities.

A	D	Y	R	I	L	O	P	K	F
F	M	C	V	N	I	M	K	G	I
C	A	T	C	H	G	D	S	I	S
S	P	R	G	F	H	Y	O	F	H
Z	X	C	V	F	T	H	G	A	Z
C	B	U	I	L	D	H	G	R	F
X	T	A	M	N	F	I	R	E	J
S	H	E	L	T	E	R	W	A	K
G	W	O	O	D	H	G	A	D	W
A	H	T	C	O	L	L	E	C	T

1 catch fish
2 ______
3 ______
4 ______
5 ______

2 What will your life be like in the future? Make predictions with *will* and *won't*. Use the ideas below or your own ideas.

- work hard
- have a dog
- look cool
- become famous
- live in an apartment
- be happy
- have lots of money
- live in a cottage

I won't live in an apartment, I'll live in a very big house.

______

3 Put the letters in the correct order to find out these people's plans for the weekend. Write the words.

1 **rahinavygpat**
Gavin is h a v i n g a p a r t y.

2 **wgimigsinongmi**
Gino is g _ _ _ _ s _ _ _ _ _ _ _ _.

3 **greshedinerisfen**
Erin is s _ _ _ _ _ her f _ _ _ _ _ _ _.

4 **vititervanghuns**
Nina is v _ _ _ _ _ _ _ _ her a _ _ _ _ _.

5 **yenisplanting**
Inge is p _ _ _ _ _ _ _ t _ _ _ _ _.

4 Use the code to write the types of holiday accommodation.

A	C	E	G	H	L	M	N	O	P	R	S	T	U	V	W
✦	□	✪	💧	%	☺	✵	☼	⌘	✈	$	❖	●	◆	?	◎

https://www.bookmyhotel.com

HOME | ACCOMMODATION | FLIGHTS | TOURS

1 ✦✈✦$●✵✪☼● apartment
2 ●✪☼● ______
3 □⌘●●✦💧✪ ______
4 □✦$✦?✦☼ ______
5 □✦✵✈✪$?✦☼ ______
6 %⌘●✪☺ ______

5 VOCABULARY BANK

Clothes

boots

cap

hoodie

jacket

jeans

joggers

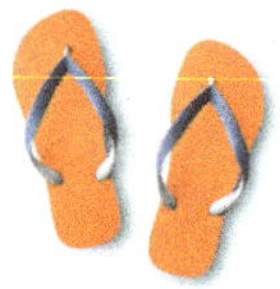
flip-flops

trainers

T-shirt

skirt

shirt

shorts

1 Circle the correct words.

1 You *usually wear / don't usually wear* a cap indoors.
2 You *wear / don't wear* socks with flip-flops.
3 You wear shorts on your *legs / feet*.
4 People often wear jeans at *home / work*.
5 People usually wear jackets or hoodies in *cool / warm* weather.
6 You wear boots on your *hands / feet*.

Accessories

belt	earrings	necklace	ring	sunglasses	wallet
bracelet	gloves	purse	scarf	umbrella	watch

2 Put the letters in order to make accessories.

1 It's sunny, so she's wearing a T-shirt and *sesglsunas* __________.
2 She always wears a gold necklace and *sarering* __________.
3 It's raining – put on your jacket and take an *umaellbr* __________.
4 When it's cold I wear my boots and *ovglse* __________.
5 Most people keep their money in a purse or a *tellwa* __________.
6 He always wears a *lebt* __________ with his jeans.

LEARN TO LEARN

Making a picture dictionary

Drawing and labelling pictures helps you remember new vocabulary.

3 Draw a person with six of the accessories above. Label the accessories.

____

____

____

____

____

____

6 VOCABULARY BANK

Sports

athletics

basketball

(mountain/ rock) climbing

gymnastics

hockey

rugby

running

sailing

swimming

table tennis

volleyball

windsurfing

yoga

1 Correct the verbs in these sentences.

1 They play ________ swimming every Wednesday after school.
2 She goes ________ gymnastics at the weekend.
3 Do you do ________ basketball?
4 I go ________ hockey at school.
5 We often play________ rock climbing in the summer.

Sport verbs

bounce	climb	hit	kick	pass	score
catch	dive	jump	lift	run	throw

2 Work with a partner. Take turns to choose a sports verb and do the action. Your partner guesses the verb and says a sport that uses it.

LEARN TO LEARN

Remembering vocabulary sets

When you learn a new word, write down other forms of the word. This improves your vocabulary.

3 Write words for people who do these sports.

1 climbing ________ climber
2 football ________
3 running ________
4 swimming ________
5 volleyball ________

7 VOCABULARY BANK

Animals

bear

crocodile

donkey

duck

eagle

giraffe

hippo

horse

lion

monkey

mouse

parrot

snake

whale

1 **Complete the categories with the animals. Some animals can go in more than one category.**

land			air	water
________	________	________	________	________
________	________	________	________	________
________	________	________	________	________
________	________	________		________

Adjectives

beautiful	cute	heavy	lazy	noisy	tiny
clever	dangerous	large	long	quiet	wild

2 **Put the letters in order to describe the animals.**

1 I saw a *eutc* ________ duck in the park.

2 There are *gealr* ________ crocodiles in the water here.

3 There was a *aubfetiul* ________ parrot in the tree.

4 Listen to that *oinys* ________ lion!

LEARN TO LEARN

Remembering new vocabulary

Using new words in a sentence helps you remember them.

3 **Write true sentences about animals. Use the adjectives above.**

1 I love mice because they are tiny and cute.

2 ________________________________

3 ________________________________

4 ________________________________

5 ________________________________

8 VOCABULARY BANK

Places in town

aquarium

bowling alley

car park

cinema

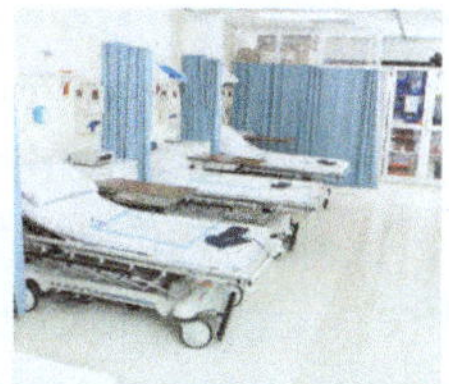
hospital

ice rink

post office

shopping centre

skate park

sports centre

swimming pool

1 Match the sentence halves.

1 I went to the post
2 There is a big shopping
3 He loves going to the bowling
4 The water in the swimming
5 We met at the ice

a alley with his friends.
b pool was very cold today.
c rink to go skating.
d office to buy some stamps.
e centre in this city.

Personal possessions

bus pass	headphones	laptop	phone
camera	ID card	money	portable charger
concert ticket	keys	passport	tablet

2 Circle the correct words.

1 I took *keys* / *money* / *headphones* to the shopping centre to buy some clothes.
2 You need a *concert ticket* / *phone* / *passport* to go to another country.
3 He used his *bus pass* / *tablet* / *portable charger* to get to the sports centre.
4 You can use *headphones* / *keys* / *cameras* to listen to music.
5 She took a *camera* / *laptop* / *ID card* to take pictures of the fish at the aquarium.

LEARN TO LEARN

Making real sentences

When you learn new words, use them to talk about your life. This will help you remember them.

3 Work in pairs. Take turns to choose a personal possession and say when, where or why you use it.

I use my tablet on the bus to watch videos.

9 VOCABULARY BANK

Outdoor life

build a shelter	find food and water	read a map
catch fish	identify plants	use a compass
collect wood	light a fire	
cook over a campfire	pick fruit	

1 Look at the outdoor life phrases and try to remember them. Cover the list. Work in pairs. Take turns to say a verb. Can your partner remember the phrase? Can you remember all ten?

pick

a shelter?

No! Pick fruit!

Holidays

apartment

B&B (bed and breakfast)

camper van

caravan

chalet

cottage

hotel

tent

youth hostel

2 Put the letters in order to make types of accommodation.

1 We stayed in an *mentparat* __________ by the sea.
2 We go to our *telcha* __________ every summer and catch fish from the lake.
3 My granny lives in a pretty *ttocgea* __________ in the country.
4 When we stay in our *nett* __________, we cook over a campfire.
5 We drove our *pecamr nav* __________ __________ to the mountains.

LEARN TO LEARN

Personalising spidergrams

Personalising a spidergram with colours or pictures can help you remember new vocabulary.

3 Make a spidergram. Write 'Types of accommodation' in the middle. Add three words for types of accommodation you want to learn and draw pictures next to the words.

6 PE

1 Discuss the questions.

1 Which sports do you do?

2 Which of these skills do you need to do your favourite sport?

bouncing	catching	jumping	kicking	teamwork

6.12 **2 Read the article. Check the meaning of the words in bold. Match them with the definitions.**

1 ________: the ability to do something difficult for a long time

2 ________: very strong

3 ________: takes part in a competition

3 Read the article again and match the sentence halves.

1 Olga and Maya are

2 Type I muscle tissue is

3 Type II muscle tissue gets

4 Maya has got

a more Type II muscle tissue than Olga.

b both runners.

c better for stamina.

d tired fast.

Explore it!

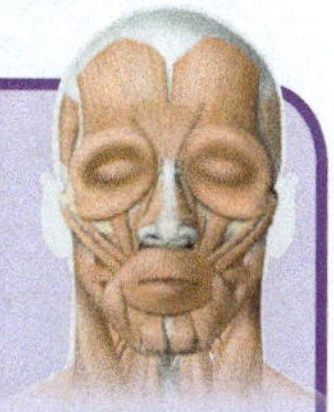

Guess the correct answer.

What's the fastest muscle in the body?

a eye   b tongue   c finger

Find an interesting fact about muscles. Write a question for your partner to answer.

FAST OR SLOW?

Meet Olympic sportspeople Olga and Maya. They have a lot in common, but they are also very different.

Olga **competes** in an event with three different parts: the triathlon. She swims 1.5 km, then cycles 40 km and finishes with a 10-km run!

Maya runs the 100-metre race. She is much faster than Olga. But she cannot do a triathlon.

Olga has got more **stamina** and Maya has got more speed. But why? What's different inside their bodies?

The difference is in the types of muscles they use.

Type I muscle tissue (slow-twitch)

This muscle doesn't have a lot of power, but it can keep going. Marathon runners use Type I muscle tissue.

Type II muscle tissue (fast-twitch)

This is much more **powerful**, but it gets tired fast – in less than a minute. Sprinters use Type II muscle tissue.

Now, the difference is obvious. Olga trains her slow-twitch muscles more and Maya has a lot more fast-twitch muscle.

So, which is better?
Which muscles have you got more of?

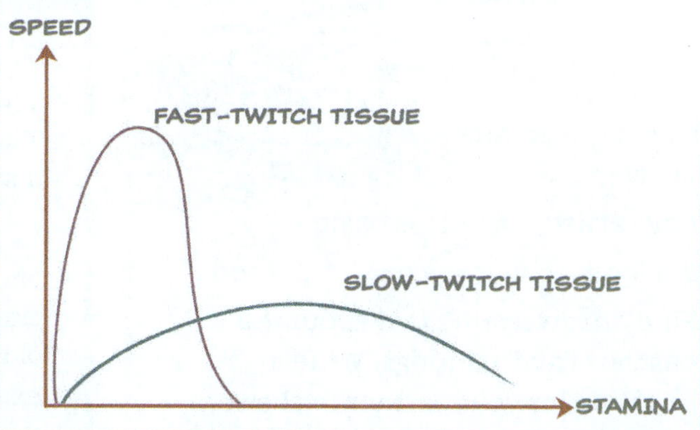

8 HISTORY

1 How old are the paintings in the picture?

8.13 2 Read the article and check your ideas in Exercise 1.

3 Find the synonyms in **bold** in the text.

1 amazing ______
2 hole ______
3 profound ______
4 something you find ______

4 Match questions a–f with paragraphs 1–6.

a What did they find?
b Did the boys keep their promise?
c Where did the boys make the discovery?
d How did the boys feel?
e When did the discovery take place?
f How did they make the discovery?

5 Read the article again and put the events in order.

a ☐ The boys saw a hole in the ground.
b ☐ Archaeologists came to see the paintings.
c ☐ The boys saw pictures of animals in a cave.
d ☐ The boys threw stones down a hole.

Explore it!

Guess the correct answer.

Cave artists used … as paint.

a blood b charcoal c food

Find an interesting fact about the Lascaux cave paintings. Write a question for your partner to answer.

The Lascaux Cave Paintings

1 ☐

On 12 September, 1940 four teenage boys made an amazing discovery. What do you think they discovered? Read on to find out …

2 ☐

The boys were in the woods near the village of Montignac, France. One of them, Marcel Ravidat, saw a hole in the ground a few days earlier. They believed it was the entrance to a secret tunnel that people in the village talked about.

3 ☐

First, they looked inside the hole. Then they threw stones through the **opening** to see how **deep** it was. They decided to go in and carefully climbed down fifteen metres. At the bottom there was a cave. They were amazed by what they saw.

4 ☐

There were **incredible** paintings all over the walls, including hundreds of pictures of red, black, brown and yellow animals. The animals looked like they were moving in the dark.

5 ☐

The boys were excited but also worried about getting out. They left the cave and promised to keep their **discovery** a secret.

6 ☐

No, the whole village soon found out, and archaeologists came to visit. The cave paintings were about 17,000 years old. Can you imagine that? They are still some of the best examples of prehistoric art ever discovered.

UNIT 5

-ing

5.03 **1 Listen and repeat.**

play**ing** stand**ing** sing**ing**

5.04 **2 Match the sentence halves. Listen, check and repeat.**

1 Martin is writing — c
2 Amir is catching
3 Ysabella is travelling
4 Oscar is dancing

a around the world.
b salsa.
c a letter.
d fish in the sea.

3 Practise saying the sentences in Exercise 2.

UNIT 6

Schwa /ə/

6.04 **1 Listen and repeat.**

better	1	faster	☐	older	☐
bigger	☐	happier	☐	smaller	☐
easier	☐	healthier	☐	smarter	☐

2 Match the words in Exercise 1 with the stress patterns. Write 1 or 2 in the box.

1 Oo 2 Ooo

6.05 **3 Listen and repeat the sentences. Write how many schwa /ə/ sounds you hear. Practise saying the sentences.**

1 Jane is smaller than her sister. 4
2 Bossaball is better than football. ☐
3 My brother is happier now he plays rugby. ☐

UNIT 7

/t/, /d/ and /ɪd/

7.06 **1 Listen and repeat.**

/t/ lik**ed** /d/ play**ed** /ɪd/ want**ed**

7.07 **2 Listen and write A (/t/ or /d/) or B (/ɪd/).**

1 looked A
2 wanted ☐
3 danced ☐
4 needed ☐

3 Write the past simple form of the verbs in the box and put them in the correct place in the table.

call climb hunt start want watch

/t/ **or** /d/	/ɪd/
called	

7.08 **4 Listen, check and repeat.**

5 Cover the table in Exercise 3 and take turns to say a verb from the box. Your partner says the past form of the verb. Check your partner's pronunciation.

UNIT 8

Intonation in questions

8.03 **1 Listen and repeat.**

1 Did Pablo move house?
2 Did they go to the swimming pool yesterday?

2 Mark where your voice goes up in the questions.

1 Did Alex play basketball at the sports centre?
2 Did you take the letter to the post office?
3 Did Fred and George buy anything?
4 Did your brother go to the library?

8.04 **3 Listen, check and repeat.**

UNIT 9

be going to

9.07 **1 Listen and repeat.**

1 What are you **going to** do?
2 I'm **gonna** watch a film.

9.08 **2 Listen and choose the option you hear. Practise saying the sentences.**

1 He's *going to* / *gonna* order pizza.
2 Are they *going to* / *gonna* travel to Turkey?
3 I'm not *going to* / *gonna* tell you the secret.
4 Are you *going to* / *gonna* help me?
5 She's *going to* / *gonna* buy a new T-shirt.
6 Is he *going to* / *gonna* talk to the teacher?

IRREGULAR VERBS

Infinitive	Past simple	Past participle
be	was / were	been
beat	beat	beaten
become	became	become
begin	began	begun
break	broke	broken
bring	brought	brought
build	built	built
buy	bought	bought
catch	caught	caught
choose	chose	chosen
come	came	come
cost	cost	cost
cut	cut	cut
do	did	done
draw	drew	drawn
drink	drank	drunk
drive	drove	driven
eat	ate	eaten
fall	fell	fallen
feel	felt	felt
fight	fought	fought
find	found	found
fly	flew	flown
forget	forgot	forgotten
get	got	got
give	gave	given
go	went	gone
grow	grew	grown
have	had	had
hear	heard	heard
hide	hid	hidden
hit	hit	hit
hold	held	held
keep	kept	kept

Infinitive	Past simple	Past participle
know	knew	known
leave	left	left
lose	lost	lost
make	made	made
meet	met	met
pay	paid	paid
put	put	put
read	read	read
ride	rode	ridden
ring	rang	rung
run	ran	run
say	said	said
see	saw	seen
sell	sold	sold
send	sent	sent
show	showed	shown
shut	shut	shut
sing	sang	sung
sit	sat	sat
sleep	slept	slept
speak	spoke	spoken
spend	spent	spent
stand	stood	stood
swim	swam	swum
take	took	taken
teach	taught	taught
tell	told	told
think	thought	thought
throw	threw	thrown
understand	understood	understood
wake	woke	woken
wear	wore	worn
win	won	won
write	wrote	written

OWN IT! 1

A2 Key test content in *Own It!* Level 1 has been checked by Cambridge Assessment English for accuracy and level.

WORKBOOK

Vicki Anderson and Lynn Durrant

CAMBRIDGE UNIVERSITY PRESS

CONTENTS

5 WHAT'S YOUR STYLE?

VOCABULARY

Clothes

1 ☆ Look at the photos and (circle) the correct words.

1 *boots* / *(trainers)*
2 *hoodie* / *T-shirt*
3 *jeans* / *joggers*
4 *boots* / *flip-flops*
5 *shorts* / *skirt*
6 *T-shirt* / *jacket*

2 ☆ Look at the picture. Complete the text with the words in the box.

boots	cap	jacket	joggers
shirt	shorts	trainers	~~T-shirt~~

Laura's favourite outfit is a 1 ___T-shirt___, 2 ______, 3 ______ and a 4 ______. Alex's favourite outfit is a 5 ______ and a 6 ______, 7 ______ and 8 ______.

3 ☆☆☆ What can you wear? Write at least three clothes items for each situation.

1 Your friends ask you to go to the mountains with them in December.

I can wear ______

2 It's July and you have a picnic with your parents.

______

3 It's Saturday afternoon and you want to visit your grandma.

______

Explore it!

Guess the correct answer.

A *kurta* is a long shirt without a collar. Men and women from *South America* / *South Asia* / *Europe* wear kurtas.

Find an interesting fact about clothes in your country. Then send a question in an email to a classmate or ask them it in the next class.

READING

An online diary

1 ☆ **Read Marina's online diary. Who doesn't like purple?**

____

Marina'sFashionFriends.com

Sunday, 10.30 am

It's Sunday morning and I'm writing this post from the park. I'm here with my family. I can see a group of girls. They're talking and having some snacks. One girl looks great! I want her clothes! She's wearing purple jeans, an orange T-shirt, a black cap and some fabulous purple trainers. I think those trainers are in a shop round the corner! Hmm … have I got the money to buy them?

14.00 pm (and back online!)

I'm at home and guess what? I've got those lovely trainers!

18.00 pm

Comments

Ethan: Hi, Marina! I always read your diary and I usually like your ideas. But sorry … I don't like purple. I think it's a horrible colour! It's a nice day today and I'm in a park, too. I'm wearing my new joggers and a T-shirt, but it's hot now and I'm not wearing my cap. What are you wearing?

Ada: Where can I buy those trainers? I want some, too. Ethan, purple is THE colour! I've got six purple T-shirts and a pair of purple shorts! I'm wearing my favourite purple T-shirt today!

20.00 pm

Ada, they're selling them in World of Trainers. I'm wearing them now!
Now I need some jeans.
Sorry, Ethan, purple is THE colour!

New post tomorrow!

2 ☆☆ **Read the diary again and underline these words. Check their meaning in a dictionary and then complete the sentences.**

corner ~~fabulous~~ guess what lovely pair

1 I love my green boots. They're __fabulous__!

2 __________? We're in the same class!

3 The clothes shop isn't far away. It's round the __________.

4 Sara's new skirt is __________. I want one!

5 You need to get a new __________ of shoes.

3 ☆☆ **Read the diary again. Circle the correct answers.**

1 It's Sunday and Marina *is* / *(isn't)* at home.

2 She likes *one girl's* / *some girls'* trainers.

3 Ethan *usually likes* / *doesn't usually like* Marina's posts.

4 Marina and *Ethan* / *Ada* want to buy the trainers.

5 Ada *has got some* / *hasn't got any* purple clothes.

6 Marina tells *Ethan* / *Ada* the name of a trainers shop.

4 ☆☆☆ **Answer the questions with your own ideas.**

1 Do you think fashion is important? Why / Why not?

____

____

2 Where do you get your ideas about what to wear? For example, from online diaries, friends, magazines, the TV, films, shops?

____

____

LANGUAGE IN ACTION

Present continuous

1 Write the words in the correct order to make sentences.

1 on TV / I'm / fashion show / a / watching
I'm watching a fashion show on TV.

2 her / She / isn't / doing / homework
______

3 the park / sitting / Marina / is / in
______

4 a / Ethan / isn't / cap / wearing
______

5 playing / We're / football
______

6 same / skirt / the / buying / They're
______

2 Complete the message with the correct form of the verb *be*.

< Back

Hi Dad! I [1] *'m* sitting on the school bus and it [2] ______ (not) moving! The bus driver [3] ______ talking on the phone and he [4] ______ (not) looking very happy. Oh, and it [5] ______ raining! Can you come? Juan [6] ______ playing football and Mum [7] ______ (not) answering the phone. Thanks, Dad!

3 What are they doing? Look at pictures 1–4 and write sentences using the words in boxes a and b.

a dance ~~read~~ ride write

b ~~a magazine~~ salsa on the board a bike

1 *He's reading a magazine.*
2 ______
3 ______
4 ______

4 Match questions 1–6 with answers a–f.

1 Are you listening to me? *b*
2 Is Anton wearing his new trainers? ☐
3 Is Claudia studying? ☐
4 What are they eating? ☐
5 Which film is Pedro watching? ☐
6 Where are you having your lunch? ☐

a *Wonder Woman*.
b ~~Yes, I am~~!
c In the canteen.
d No, she isn't.
e Fried spiders. Yuck!
f Yes, he is.

5 Answer the questions.

1 What are you wearing today?
______

2 What is your best friend doing now?
______

6 Find out what two people in your family are doing now. Write sentences in the present continuous.

My sister's watching TV.
______
______
______

1

2

3

4

VOCABULARY AND LISTENING

Accessories

1 ☆ **Complete the accessory words in the spidergram.**

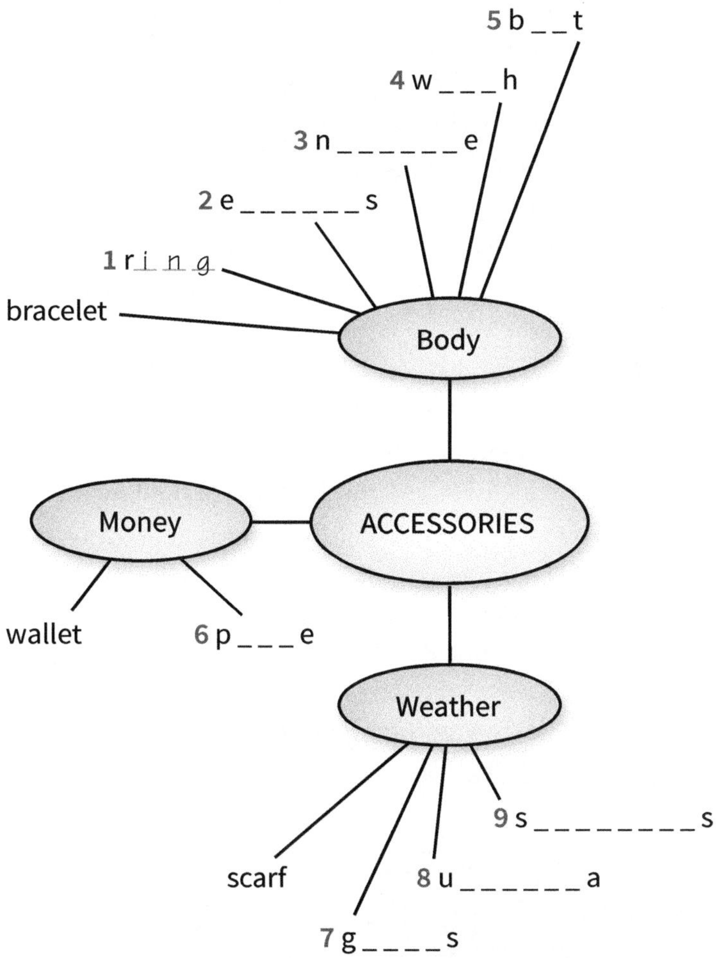

2 ☆☆ **Complete the sentences with words from Exercise 1.**

1 Those new jeans look big. You need a *belt* .

2 José always wears ______________ when it's sunny.

3 Miriam doesn't use a wallet for her money. She uses a ______________ .

4 I don't wear a ______________ because there's a clock in the classroom.

5 It's raining and I haven't got my ______________ !

6 In cold weather, my grandma always wears ______________ and a ______________ .

7 My dad has a big ______________ , but he's never got any money in it!

An interview

5.01 **3** ☆ **Listen to the interview. Tick (✓) the two things that Alba paints.**

1
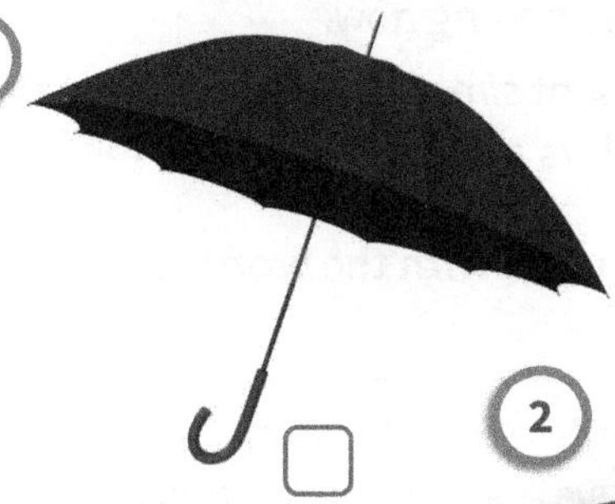
☐

2
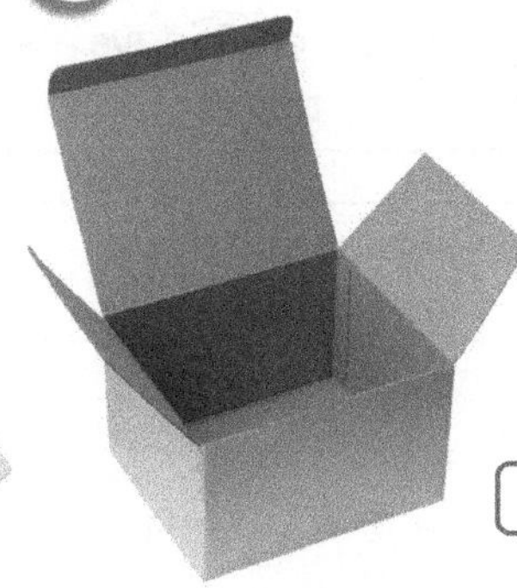
☐

3

☐

5.01 **4** ☆☆☆ **Listen again. Answer the questions.**

1 Who is Alba painting this week?
Her baby brother.

2 Where does she get her ideas from?
____

3 What does she put in the mini boxes?
____

4 What is inside the box for her friend?
____

5 What does the interviewer want?
____

5 ☆ **Alba is making you a box (big or small). Write two things you want to put in it. Use the ideas below or your own ideas.**

a bracelet a ring a wallet a watch gloves

I'd like ______________ and ______________ .

LANGUAGE IN ACTION

Present simple and present continuous

1 ☆ **Circle the correct options.**

1 We use the present *simple* / *continuous* to talk about things happening now.

2 We use the present *simple* / *continuous* to talk about facts, habits and routines.

2 ☆ **Complete the table with the words and phrases in the box.**

at the moment every Monday never now ~~on Fridays~~ sometimes this week this morning today usually

Facts, habits and routines	Things happening now
on Fridays	

3 ☆☆ **Write sentences with the present simple or present continuous.**

1 Some people / wear / sports clothes / at the weekend

Some people wear sports clothes at the weekend.

2 I / look for / some jeans / right now

3 They / make / the costumes for the show / now

4 Naima / usually / buy / red clothes

5 We / never / go shopping / on Saturdays

6 A lot of people / wear / hats / at the moment

4 ☆☆ **Complete the conversation with the present simple or present continuous form of the verbs in brackets.**

DANA What [1] *are you doing* (do), Paula?

PAULA I [2] ______ (look) at my clothes. Some of them are very small now. I [3] ______ (often / need) new clothes in the summer.

DANA Oh! Can I have this skirt?

PAULA Well, I [4] ______ (always / give) my small clothes to my little sister, but she [5] ______ (not wear) skirts, so it's yours!

DANA Thanks! Where [6] ______ (you / usually / buy) your clothes?

PAULA A shop near home. My mum [7] ______ (shop) there right now.

DANA [8] ______ (they / sell) accessories, too? I [9] ______ (look for) a bracelet at the moment.

PAULA Yes, they do! They [10] ______ (sell) lovely bracelets. We can go shopping there together next time!

5 ☆☆☆ **Answer the questions.**

1 What do you do with your old clothes and accessories?

2 What clothes are you wearing a lot at the moment?

3 What do you usually wear in the evening during the week?

WRITING

A description of a photo

1 ☆ **Read the description and look at the photo. Write the names of the people (a–e).**

a ___Damir___ d ________
b ________ e ________
c ________

2 ☆☆ **Circle the correct form of the verbs (1–7) in the description.**

3 ☆☆ **Read the description again. Complete the sentences with the words in the box.**

Alyssa	boys	girls	Peter	~~trees~~

1 The ___trees___ are at the back.
2 ________ is in the middle. Carmen and ________ are next to her.
3 The ________ are on the left.
4 The ________ are on the right.

4 ☆☆ **Match topics a–c with paragraphs 1–3.**

a why it is a favourite photo ☐
b people in the photo, where they are, what they're wearing ☐
c who is in the photo and where the photo is ☐

A photo of a day out
By Alyssa

1 This is a photo of my friends and me. We're on a school trip to a national park. It's cold but sunny.

2 The boy on the left is Damir. He [1]*looks* / *'s looking* down. He often [2]*looks* / *is looking* down because he hates photos! He [3]*wears* / *'s wearing* a black and grey hoodie. Next to Damirl is Peter. He's in a pink shirt and a grey jumper. The boys [4]*don't wear* / *aren't wearing* jackets in the photo. Then that's me in the middle, with a jacket and a checked shirt. Carmen's next to me. She [5]*wears* / *'s wearing* her favourite denim jacket and a big scarf. Gina's on the right. She's got a grey T-shirt, a green jacket and a scarf. Gina's the only one in a hat.

3 This is one of my favourite photos. We [6]*laugh* / *'re laughing* because it's a fun day. I like this photo because there are trees at the back and we all look happy. We always [7]*have* / *are having* a great time!

Write your own description of a photo of a day out.

PLAN

5 ☆☆ **Choose your photo and make notes. Decide what information to include in each paragraph. Use the information in Exercise 4 to help you.**

WRITE

6 ☆☆☆ **Write your description. Remember to include the information in the correct order, the present simple and present continuous, and expressions from the *Useful language* box (see Student's Book, p65).**

CHECK

7 **Do you ...**

- describe the people in the photo, including the clothes and accessories they are wearing?
- describe the people's positions in the photo?
- say why you like the photo?

5 REVIEW

VOCABULARY

1 Circle the odd one out.

1 joggers / T-shirt / jeans
2 trainers / shorts / boots
3 shorts / boots / skirt
4 jacket / hoodie / cap
5 shirt / skirt / shorts
6 flip-flops / boots / trainers

2 Complete the crossword. Use the pictures.

ACROSS →

3

6
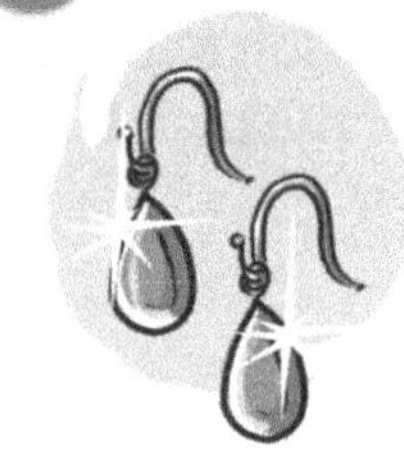
8

9
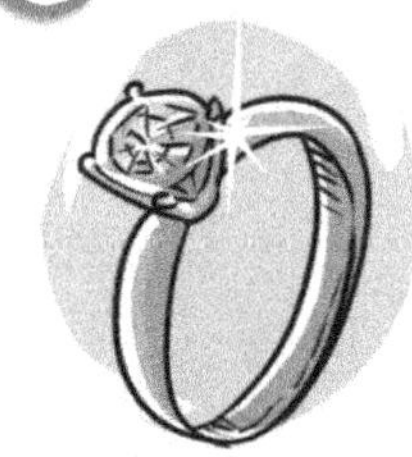
10
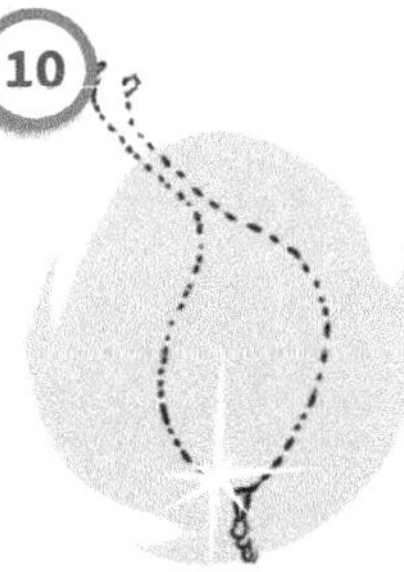
11

DOWN ↓

1

2
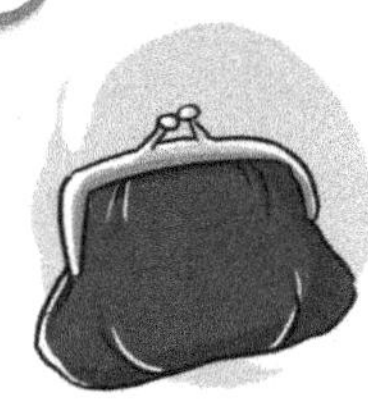
4

5

7

8

LANGUAGE IN ACTION

3 Complete the sentences with the present continuous form of the verbs in the box.

do look make not rain not wear watch

1 **A:** What ________ you ________ now?
B: I'm doing my homework.
2 At the moment, I ________ for a new jacket with my dad.
3 They ________ a TV programme about the history of fashion.
4 We ________ our school uniform today – it's Sunday.
5 My grandma ________ me a new dress for my birthday.
6 You don't need an umbrella. It ________.

4 Circle the correct options.

MAYA What [1]*do you usually do / are you usually doing* at the weekend?

ISAAC We [2]*sometimes visit / are sometimes visiting* my grandparents, but they [3]*travel / 're travelling* around Europe at the moment.

LILY [4]*Is Jimi having / Does Jimi have* lunch at home this month?

TOM Yes. He usually [5]*has / is having* lunch at school, but this month he [6]*goes / 's going* home early.

HUGO [7]*Does Dad do / Is Dad doing* the shopping now?

CALEB No, it's Sunday. The shops [8]*close / are closing* early on Sundays.

CUMULATIVE LANGUAGE

5 Complete the conversation with the missing words. Circle the correct options.

ADIL Hi, Mum. [1] ________ are you?

MUM Hi, Adil! I'm [2] ________ the shopping with Dad.

ADIL Oh, OK! Listen, [3] ________ for a bike ride this afternoon with Tom and his brother?

MUM Sure! We haven't got [4] ________ plans.

ADIL Great! But [5] ________ a problem. I can't [6] ________ my trainers, or my hoodie. Where are they?

MUM I [7] ________ know. They're your things.

ADIL Oh! The trainers are under my bed, but I can't see my hoodie. Can you buy [8] ________ a new one, please?

MUM A new one? I haven't got [9] ________ time now, and you've got a hoodie! You need to look for [10] ________.

ADIL Ugh! I hate [11] ________ things.

MUM I know, but how often [12] ________ things when you look for them?

ADIL Hmm, I suppose so. OK, speak later.

	a	b	c
1	When	Where	What
2	does	do	doing
3	can I go	I can go	do I go
4	any	some	a
5	there are	there's	it's
6	find	to find	finding
7	not	'm not	don't
8	me	it	my
9	many	any	a lot
10	it	they	them
11	look for	looking for	looks for
12	are you finding	do you find	you find

6 SPORT FOR LIFE

VOCABULARY

Sports

1 ★ **Complete the word puzzle. Use the pictures (1–12). What is the mystery word in grey?**

2 ★★ **Complete the rules with *play*, *do* or *go*.**

We usually use [1] ________ with sports that end in *-ing*.

We usually use [2] ________ with ball sports.

We usually use [3] ________ with other sports.

3 ★★ **Circle the correct options.**

I like doing sport. At school, we do [1]*running* / *athletics* and I like that. Sometimes at the weekend I go [2]*swimming* / *yoga* with my brother. He does [3]*gymnastics* / *rugby* at an after-school club and goes [4]*running* / *table tennis* twice a week. I don't really like team sports, but in the holidays I sometimes play [5]*sailing* / *volleyball* with my friends on the beach. And I love going [6]*yoga* / *rock climbing* with my dad in the mountains.

4 ★★★ **Answer the questions.**

1 What are your favourite sports?

____

2 Do you do sports at school? Which sports?

____

Explore it!

Guess the correct answer.

Which sport comes from Canada?

a ice hockey b table tennis c rugby

Find an interesting fact about sport in your country. Then send a question in an email to a classmate or ask them it in the next class.

READING
Online FAQs

1 ☆ **Read the article. What sport is it about? Tick (✓) the correct photo (1–3).**

1
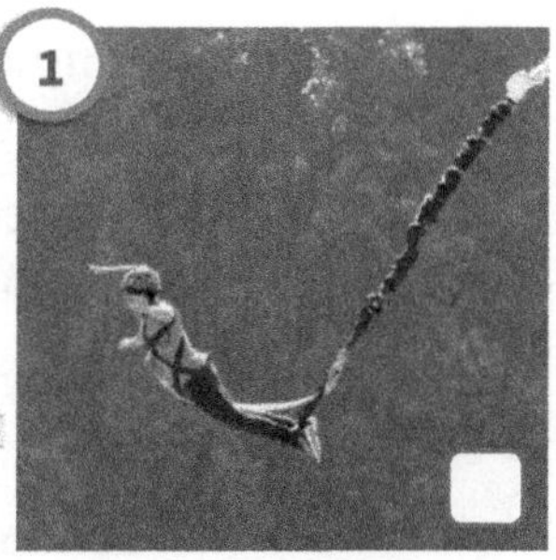

2

3

FUN IN THE SUN!

Are you looking for a new sport? Do you want to try something more exciting? In New Zealand we've got the answer – try zorbing! It's new and it's different!

FAQs

Q1:
What is Zorbing?

Zorbing is a fun outdoor sport. It's more popular here in New Zealand than in other countries.

Q2: __________

You need a large plastic ball. This is called a zorb. You get inside the ball and run or walk. When you move, the ball moves, too! You know where you're going and how you're moving because you can see through the ball. Lots of people love going down a hill in their zorb. It's exciting!

Q3: __________

No, it's an individual sport. You get inside the zorb on your own, but it's good fun to go with family or friends because you can have races – sometimes children are faster than their parents!

Q4: __________

Yes, it is, but always do it in a zorbing centre and follow the rules. Have fun, but be careful – don't get hurt!

Q5: __________

Yes. To go zorbing, you usually need to be six years old or older.

Q6: __________

There are zorbing centres in many places on the South Island. Click here for a list of centres.

Q7: __________

Yes, it's more expensive than other traditional sports, but it's a great activity for special days. So, are you ready for zorbing? What are you waiting for!

2 ☆☆ **Read the article again. Complete it with the missing questions.**

a Is there an age limit?
b Is it a team sport?
c What do you do?
d ~~What is zorbing~~?
e Where can I do it?
f Is it expensive?
g Is it safe?

3 ☆☆ **Read the article again and <u>underline</u> these words. Then check their meaning in a dictionary and complete the sentences.**

get hurt hill race ~~safe~~ try

1 Be careful! Going out alone at night isn't *safe*.
2 The Spartathlon is a __________ in Greece. People run 246 kilometres!
3 I live at the top of a __________. Walking down to school is easy!
4 I love tennis, but this year I want to __________ a new sport.
5 Careful there! You can fall and __________!

4 ☆☆☆ **Answer the questions.**

1 Do you want to try zorbing? Why / Why not?

____

2 What fun outdoor sports are popular in your country?

____

LANGUAGE IN ACTION
Comparatives

1 ★ Write the comparative forms.

1 small smaller
2 big ______
3 good ______
4 happy ______
5 interesting ______
6 bad ______

2 ★ Complete the rules with the adjectives from Exercise 1.

1 For one-syllable adjectives, add *-er*: smaller.
2 For two-syllable adjectives ending in *-y*, remove the *-y* and add *-ier*: ______.
3 For long adjectives, add *more* to the adjective: ______.
4 For one-syllable adjectives ending in a vowel and a consonant, double the consonant and add *-er*: ______.
5 For irregular adjectives, use a different word: ______ and ______.

3 ★★ Underline and correct one mistake in each sentence.

1 Windsurfing is more expensive <u>that</u> running. than
2 Rugby is more fast than basketball. ______
3 Runners are usually thiner than swimmers. ______
4 Which sport is noisyer, volleyball or yoga? ______
5 She's badder at gymastics than at hockey. ______
6 Playing sport is more better than watching it. ______

4 ★★ Complete the sentences with the comparative form of the adjectives in brackets.

1 An ice hockey match is longer than a basketball match. (long)
2 I think rock climbing is ______ than yoga. (exciting)
3 Lola's ______ at tennis than her dad. (good)
4 Our school hockey team is ______ than the rugby team. (bad)
5 We think rugby is a ______ game than football. (difficult)
6 Doing sport is ______ than watching TV. (healthy)

5 ★★ Complete the questions with a comparative adjective. Then check the answers at the bottom of the page.

DANIEL Let's do this quiz! First question: Which ball is [1] faster, a table tennis or a tennis ball?
ANDREA A table tennis ball?
DANIEL Next question: Which match is [2] ______, a basketball or an ice hockey match?
ANDREA I don't know. Ice hockey?
DANIEL Number three: Which country is [3] ______ at table tennis, China or South Korea?
ANDREA South Korea, I think.
DANIEL And the last question: Which sport is [4] ______ at schools here in New Zealand, hockey or athletics?
ANDREA Oh, dear! I don't know. Athletics maybe. What are the answers?

6 ★★★ Write three sentences comparing sports. Look at Exercise 4 to help you.

I think football is more entertaining than rugby.
______
______
______

Answers

1 table tennis ball: 116 km/h; tennis ball: 263 km/h
2 ice hockey match: 60 minutes; basketball match: 48 minutes
3 China (1); South Korea (2)
4 number of people playing at schools in New Zealand: hockey: 13,967, athletics: 12,713

VOCABULARY AND LISTENING

Sports verbs

1 ☆ **Match photos 1–6 with six of the sports verbs a–l.**

a dive b kick ~~c bounce~~ d hit e catch f climb g jump h lift i pass j run k throw l score

1

2

3

4

5

6

2 ☆☆ **Circle the correct verbs.**

I don't understand rugby! OK, the players [1]*pass* / *score* the ball to each other. Then they [2]*catch* / *run* up the field and put the ball over a line to [3]*score* / *hit* points. They also [4]*kick* / *jump* the ball over a big goalpost. But sometimes the teams make a circle and push each other. Then one player [5]*scores* / *throws* the ball into the circle and another player from the same team gets it. And sometimes some players [6]*lift* / *jump* on top of other players!

3 ☆☆☆ **Write two sentences describing what players can and can't do in a sport. Use the sports verbs from Exercise 1.**

In football, the players can kick the ball but they can't score goals with their hands.

____

____

____

A conversation

6.01 **4** ☆ **Look at the photo and listen to a conversation about goalball, a sport for blind people. Circle the correct answers.**

1 Goalball players use a special ball with *lights* / *sound*.
2 Goalball is *a team* / *an individual* sport.

6.01 **5** ☆☆☆ **Listen again. Complete the sentences with one word.**

1 Blind people can usually hear sounds ___better___ than other people.
2 The goalball ball is like a __________, but heavier.
3 A goalball team has __________ players in it.
4 Players try to __________ the ball to score a goal.
5 They use their __________ to stop the ball.
6 Some players throw the ball at __________ kilometres per hour.
7 Jon plays goalball on a __________ court.
8 The boy wants to watch Jon's match on __________.

6 ☆☆☆ **Watch part of a Paralympics goalball match on the internet. Then write three things you like about it.**

I like how the players throw the ball.

____

____

____

LANGUAGE IN ACTION

Superlatives

1 ☆ **Complete the table with the superlative form of the adjectives in the box.**

bad ~~entertaining~~ fit healthy old

The most + adjective	*The* + double the final consonant + *-est*	*The* + change *y* to *i* + *-est*	*The* + adjective + *-est*	*The* + irregular form
the most popular	2 ______	the easiest	4 ______	the best
1 the most entertaining	the biggest	3 ______	the fastest	5 ______

2 ☆☆ **Complete the text with the superlative form of the adjectives in brackets.**

My cousin Nick is the 1 most popular (popular) person in my family. He's the 2 ______ (tall) of my cousins and also the 3 ______ (fit) – at the weekend, he does yoga and plays hockey! Everybody loves Nick.

He's the 4 ______ (happy) person I know! I'm the 5 ______ (young) person in my family and the 6 ______ (bad) at sport! But that's OK because we're all different. I love reading and writing stories. Nick says I write the 7 ______ (interesting) stories in the world.

3 ☆☆ **Write the questions in the quiz using the superlative form of the adjectives. Then circle the correct answers. Check your answers at the bottom of the quiz!**

SPORTS QUESTION TIME!

1 Which is / popular / sport in Brazil?
Which is the most popular sport in Brazil?
a basketball **b** football

2 Which is one of the / old / ball sports?
______
a Ulama. It comes from Mexico.
b Alama. It comes from Ecuador.

3 Which is one of the / new / sports?
______
a table tennis.
b 360Ball. You use a racket and a ball and play it in a round field.

4 Which is one of the / difficult / sports for many people?
______
a rock climbing **b** running

5 Which is one of the / expensive / sports in the world?
______
a tennis **b** swimming

ANSWERS
1 b **2** a **3** b **4** a **5** a

4 ☆☆☆ **Complete the questions with the superlative form of the adjectives. Then answer them for you.**

1 Who is the youngest (young) person in your family?
______

2 Which is ______ (popular) sport at your school?
______

3 Which is ______ (difficult) school subject?
______

4 Which is ______ (entertaining) film you know?
______

WRITING

A profile of a sportsperson

1 ☆ **Look at the photos and read the profile. Then complete the sentence.**

For Ivan, Natalia Partyka is an ______________ sportsperson because she plays table tennis with ______________.

A popular sportsperson from my country

By Ivan Nowak

1 I'm from Poland and I think one of the [1]*more / most* popular sportspeople from my country is Natalia Partyka. She's a table tennis player. She's 1.73 m tall and weighs 64 kg. She's only got one hand and part of her right arm.

2 Natalia trains for about six hours a day. She often plays with her [2]*older / more older* sister, Sandra. Sometimes she practises bouncing the ball on the top part of her arm to begin the game. In her free time, Natalia loves reading the letters from her fans. She also likes going to the beach with her friends.

3 I think Natalia is the [3]*more / most* amazing sportsperson from my country because she plays with one hand. She's also an excellent athlete – she's part of the Paralympic team and the Olympic Games team, too. She's got more gold medals than any other table tennis player in Poland and she's one of the [4]*most / more* successful players in the world, too.

2 ☆☆ **Circle the correct options (1–4) in the profile.**

3 ☆☆ **Read the profile again. Underline two sentences with *also* and two sentences with *too*. Then complete the rules with *also* or *too*.**

We use *too* and *also* to give extra information. We use [1]________ at the end of a sentence. We use [2]________ after the verb *be* and before other verbs.

4 ☆☆ **Read the profile again. Match topics a–c with paragraphs 1–3.**

a training and other interests ☐
b achievements ☐
c basic information and description ☐

Write a profile of a popular sportsperson from your country.

PLAN

5 ☆☆ **Make notes about the sportsperson. Decide what information to include in each paragraph. Use the information in Exercise 4 to help you.**

WRITE

6 ☆☆☆ **Write your profile. Remember to include three paragraphs, comparatives and superlatives and expressions from the *Useful language* box (see Student's Book, p77).**

CHECK

7 **Do you …**

- give basic information and a description of your sportsperson?
- describe their sport using sports verbs?
- talk about their achievements and why you like them?

6 REVIEW

VOCABULARY

1 Complete the table with the sports in the box.

athletics hockey rugby
running sailing swimming tennis
windsurfing yoga

Water sports	Ball sports	Other sports
______	______	______
______	______	______
______	______	______

2 Find 12 sports verbs in the word search.

B	D	I	B	T	D	I	V	E	H
U	I	C	S	D	Q	H	G	R	I
V	O	L	I	F	T	A	H	B	T
Y	K	I	C	K	R	Z	O	S	P
E	C	M	W	Q	M	N	S	C	A
N	P	B	O	U	N	C	E	O	L
L	Y	K	J	C	J	A	T	R	U
T	H	R	O	W	V	T	G	E	R
H	J	U	M	P	W	C	E	F	U
F	P	A	S	S	K	H	X	G	N

3 Complete the sentences with the correct form of the verbs from Exercise 2.

1 A table tennis player b______ the ball across the table.
2 My brother loves j______ on the bed!
3 Mount Everest, the highest mountain in the world, is very difficult to c______.
4 We never s______ many goals in football.
5 Tennis players can't h______ the ball with their hands. They use a racket.
6 In gymnastics, we sometimes l______ heavy boxes to make our arms strong.

LANGUAGE IN ACTION

4 Write sentences using the comparative form of the adjectives in brackets.

1 zorbing / running (exciting)
______
2 water / fizzy drinks (healthy)
______
3 joggers / jeans (comfortable)
______
4 a table tennis ball / a tennis ball (small)
______
5 jumping / rock climbing (easy)
______

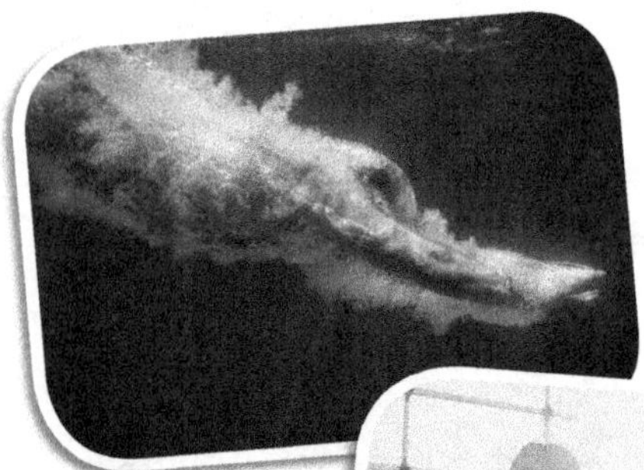

5 Complete the text with the superlative form of the adjectives in brackets.

I think tennis is the [1] ______________ (boring) sport, but my dad loves it! At the moment, he's in London at the All England Club. This club is the [2] ______________ (old) in the world. Every year, there are different tennis tournaments there. The [3] ______________ (popular) one is called Wimbledon. My dad says all the [4] ______________ (good) players want to win there. People watching tennis at Wimbledon don't usually speak to each other a lot. The [5] ______________ (bad) thing you can do at Wimbledon is talk! The players don't like noise. I think the [6] ______________ (easy) thing is to watch Wimbledon on TV, but not for me – I prefer a good film!

CUMULATIVE LANGUAGE

6 Complete the conversation with the missing words. Circle the correct options.

ESMA Which sports [1] ______________ you like, Rafael?

RAFAEL I like [2] ______________ athletics and playing football.

ESMA I think football is the [3] ______________ sport in the world.

RAFAEL Me, too! Today I [4] ______________ football training and then yoga.

ESMA Yoga! I think it's [5] ______________ than athletics!

RAFAEL Then try it with me! I can teach you the [6] ______________ exercises.

ESMA Sounds great, but I'm the [7] ______________ student in the world!

RAFAEL Ah! But I'm a [8] ______________ teacher!

ESMA OK! I [9] ______________ try.

RAFAEL [10] ______________ your joggers in your bag?

ESMA No, but I can [11] ______________ home and get them now.

RAFAEL Perfect. Run home and bring [12] ______________ joggers!

	a	b	c
1	does	are	do
2	does	do	doing
3	best	better	good
4	got	've got	'm got
5	most interesting	more interesting	interesting
6	more easy	easier	easiest
7	bad	worse	worst
8	good	the better	best
9	can	have	do
10	Have you got	You got	You have
11	go to	go	come
12	yours	you	your

7 AMAZING ANIMALS

VOCABULARY

Animals

1 Find 13 more words for animals in the word search.

C	R	O	C	O	D	I	L	E	D	E	Y
H	I	P	P	O	B	D	O	N	K	E	Y
J	L	S	I	S	W	A	Y	U	K	A	G
P	H	W	B	C	N	G	D	N	T	G	I
A	M	H	E	K	M	A	N	I	J	L	R
R	Q	O	A	V	I	D	K	T	H	E	A
R	K	R	R	P	L	U	Z	E	B	C	F
O	R	S	O	E	N	C	D	W	V	E	F
T	X	E	G	T	W	K	M	O	U	S	E
Z	F	W	H	A	L	E	S	K	S	B	A
A	N	F	M	P	B	M	O	N	K	E	Y
L	I	O	N	S	T	C	N	U	I	J	X

2 Circle the animal in each category which is not correct. Then add a different animal to each category in the list.

1 **Birds**	2 **Mammals**	3 **Reptiles**
duck	eagle	snake
hippo	giraffe	bear
parrot	lion	crocodile
______	______	______

3 Read the descriptions and write the names of the animals from Exercise 1.

1 This animal is a mammal. It usually lives in forests and cold places. It's very big and has lots of hair. *bear*

2 This animal lives in water in hot countries. It's a reptile with a big mouth and lots of big teeth. ______

3 This is a bird. It eats plants and it can swim and fly. It usually lives near water. ______

4 This animal likes cheese a lot but it doesn't like cats! It's usually grey and has lots of babies. ______

5 This animal eats meat. It hasn't got any legs. Some of them can kill other animals and sometimes people, too. ______

6 This is a very large sea mammal. It has a hole on the top of its head. ______

4 Choose another animal from Exercise 1 and write a definition.

1 This animal is ______

Explore it!

Guess the correct answer.

Which bird sometimes sleeps with an eye open?

a duck b parrot c eagle

Find another interesting fact about birds. Then send a question in an email to a classmate or ask them it in the next class.

READING

Fact files

1 ☆ **Read the fact file below and circle the correct answers.**

1 Polar bears weigh …
   a about 360 kg. b about 560 kg.

2 Polar bears live in …
   a the Arctic. b the Antarctic.

3 Polar bears eat … of seal in a week.
   a about 35 kg b about 55 kg

POLAR BEAR

Weight: about 360 kg
Habitat: the Arctic
Food: seals
Fact: Polar bears can smell a seal 32 km away! They can eat 55 kg of seal in a week.

2 ☆ **Read the article. What's special about the town of Churchill?** ______

3 ☆☆ **Read the article again and underline these words. Then check their meaning in a dictionary and complete the sentences.**

attack	escape	hunt	~~ice~~	male	prison

1 In winter, there is ___ice___ on the river.
2 A female animal is a girl and a ______ is a boy.
3 People can go to ______ for killing an elephant.
4 Hungry lions are dangerous and they sometimes ______ people.
5 Whales often ______ other mammals, like seals, at night.
6 The man saw the polar bear in the street and ran into a shop to ______.

Polar bears are in town!

Churchill is a small town on the Hudson Bay in Canada. Every October, November and December, it has some special visitors: polar bears! They can't hunt seals until it is colder and there is more ice, so they visit the town looking for food.

From October to December in 2016, there were 800 people living in Churchill and 10,000 tourists. The tourists were there to see the polar bears – there were more than 1,000 bears.

Some bears attack people, so the police ask people to be careful and to leave their cars open in the town centre. Then people can jump inside if they need to escape an angry bear! To keep people safe, the police sometimes put angry bears in prison for a few days. Then they take them out of the town.

People in the town say the worst year was 1983. On 29th November, a young male bear killed a man in the city centre. This was the first attack for many years. In 2013, a large bear attacked a man in the street. The bear was put in prison and the man went to the doctor's, but he was fine after a few days.

4 ☆☆☆ **Read the article again. Are the sentences *T* (true) or *F* (false)? Correct the false sentences.**

1 Polar bears visit the town every August.
   F. Polar bears visit the town from October to December.
2 The polar bears go to the town because it's colder there.
   ______
3 When the polar bears are angry, people can hide in cars.
   ______
4 When the polar bears attack people, they go to prison.
   ______

5 ☆☆☆☆ **Answer the questions with your own ideas.**

1 What do you think the polar bears eat in Churchill?
   ______
2 Do you think the food they eat in Churchill is good for them? Why / Why not?
   ______

LANGUAGE IN ACTION

was/were, there was/were

1 ★ Circle the correct options.

1 The polar bears *was* / *were* in Churchill in November because *there wasn't* / *there weren't* enough food for them to eat in the river.

2 In the past, the weather *was* / *were* always cold in November and *there was* / *there were* a lot of ice on the river.

3 When it *was* / *were* colder, *there was* / *there were* seals for the polar bears to eat in the river.

4 In the past *there was* / *there were* more ice because the temperatures *wasn't* / *weren't* as high.

2 ★ Match the questions with the answers.

1 Was it hotter in the past? ☐ a Yes, there were.

2 Were they wild animals? ☐ b No, there wasn't.

3 Was there ice in summer? ☐ c Yes, they were.

4 Were there seals? ☐ d No, it wasn't.

3 ★★ Complete the text with *was(n't)* / *were(n't)*.

Thousands of years ago there were mammoths in Europe. They [1] *were* large mammals with very big tusks. They [2] ________ very strong. They [3] ________ like the elephants we see today because they [4] ________ much bigger and had fur. The sabre-toothed tiger also lived in Europe at the same time. It [5] ________ really a tiger, it [6] ________ a big cat. Its teeth [7] ________ very long and it [8] ________ a very dangerous animal.

4 ★★ Complete the text with the correct form of *there was* or *there were*.

When I was a girl, I lived in South Africa. Around my house [1] *there wasn't* a lot to do but [2] ________ lots of animals to see because we lived next to a wildlife park. In my bedroom [3] ________ a big window, and in the mornings, I could see lots of animals. [4] ________ hippos in the water and [5] ________ enormous elephants sleeping. [6] ________ always a big giraffe next to a tree and a strange bird sitting on the tree that looked angry! My favourite animals are tigers, but [7] ________ any tigers in the wildlife park. That's because there are no tigers in South Africa. [8] ________ a lot of time to see the animals because I was at school all day, but I remember all of them.

5 ★★ Put the words in the correct order to make questions. Then write answers for you in your notebook.

1 were / Where / on Saturday / you / ?

Where were you on Saturday?

2 your / favourite / six / What / was / animal / when / you / were / ?

What was ________

3 people / were / there / How / many / last year / your / class / in / ?

How many ________

4 in 2011 / were / you / How / old / ?

How old ________

5 your town / in / Was / there / were / you / when / young / a zoo / ?

Was there ________

6 ★★★ Find out about an animal from the past, like mammoths or sabre-toothed tigers. Write three sentences about them. Use *was* and *were*.

____

____

____

VOCABULARY AND LISTENING

Adjectives

1 ★ Choose the correct letters to complete the adjectives.

a	c	d	~~f~~	g	i	l	n	r	u	v	y

1 beauti*f*ul
2 cle__er
3 __ute
4 dan__erous
5 heav__
6 l__zy
7 wil__
8 no__sy
9 ti__y
10 la__ge
11 q__iet
12 __ong

2 ★★ Complete the text with adjectives from Exercise 1.

I've got a ¹ *beautiful* little cat. He's got a lovely face and I think he's really ²________. He's ³________ too and can do lots of tricks. My mum likes him because he doesn't make a lot of noise like some pets. She says he's very ⁴________. He can't run fast because his legs aren't very ⁵________! I prefer small pets because some of my friends' big pets are ⁶________ and they make me nervous.

3 ★★★ Which pets have your family or friends got? Use the adjectives and your own ideas to write four sentences.

My best friend has got a tiny mouse.

____

____

____

____

A class discussion

7.01 4 ★ Listen to a teacher talking about wolves with her class. Circle the correct answers.

1 The teacher is talking about wolves that live in an *American park* / *English zoo*.
2 There weren't any wolves there for *50* / *70* years.
3 There were about *6* / *100* wolves there last year.

7.01 5 ★★ Listen again and answer the questions. Remember the *Learn to Learn* tip: look for the question words and think about the answers before you listen.

1 How does one student describe wolves?
They are fast, dangerous and clever.

2 Why weren't there any wolves in Yellowstone Park for 70 years?
____

3 How many wolves were in the park about 20 years ago?
____

4 Why was it difficult for the wolves at first?
____

5 Why is it difficult to see wolves in the park?
____

6 ★★★ Which other wild animals do you think live in Yellowstone Park? Write some ideas below.

____

LANGUAGE IN ACTION

Past simple: regular and irregular verbs

1 Write the infinitive of these past tense verbs.

1 had _have_
2 slept ______
3 took ______
4 looked ______
5 heard ______
6 saw ______
7 became ______
8 gave ______
9 shared ______
10 wanted ______
11 found ______
12 went ______

2 Complete the sentences with the correct past simple form of the verbs in the box.

look ~~not give~~ have not want sleep not find see not go

1 You _didn't give_ the donkey its food.
2 We ______ lots of snakes at the wildlife park.
3 The horse ______ to eat my apple. It wasn't hungry.
4 They ______ for the cat in the garden but they ______ him.
5 My dad ______ a parrot as a pet when he was a child.
6 The cat ______ out, she ______ on my bed all day.

3 Write the words in the correct order to make sentences.

1 park / years / The / 20 / safari / opened / ago
The safari park opened 20 years ago.
2 Crocodiles / killed / year / 1,000 / people / last
______
3 bears / days / in town / ago / Two / three / were / there
______
4 blue / last / saw / whales / summer / They
______
5 an / The / home / hour / cat / came / ago
______

4 Complete the text with the past simple form of the verbs in brackets.

Flo, a dog from Northern Ireland, disappeared in October 2011. The Gallaghers, Flo's family, [1] _looked_ (look) for her but they [2] ______ (not find) her. They were very sad. Then in 2014, a volunteer at the local animal hospital [3] ______ (hear) about a dog with no home. The dog [4] ______ (sleep) in an old building about ten miles from the Gallaghers' house. The volunteers at the hospital [5] ______ (not want) the dog to stay there. They [6] ______ (go) to find her. Soon the dog [7] ______ (have) a new home at the animal hospital, and they [8] ______ (share) photos of her on Facebook. The Gallagher family [9] ______ (see) the photos and [10] ______ (become) very excited – it was Flo! The next day they [11] ______ (take) her home. They [12] ______ (give) her a big dinner.

WRITING

A biography

1 ☆ **Look at the photos and read the biography. Which animals did Jack help?**

____

Jack Oliver

1 Jack Oliver was born in Australia [1]in / on 1978. His family started an animal sanctuary to give animals a safe place to live. [2]*When / At* Jack was five, he found a three-metre snake in his garden! It was injured! Jack and his parents decided to look after it. Jack helped at the sanctuary and he became an animal expert.

2 Jack met his wife Alison [3]*on / in* 2003. They had a daughter called Ava. [4]*In / On* 2005, Jack started to make TV programmes with a local TV channel. He filmed several series at his family's sanctuary. He also went to other countries to find and help injured animals. He helped to make them better and find a safe place for them to live. [5]*In / On* 25th September, 2012, Jack had an accident with a crocodile but he survived.

3 Jack's wife and daughter help with his work. A few weeks [6]*when / ago*, Ava found an injured duck and decided to take it to her father's sanctuary. She helped her father to look after it. Ava wants to be an animal expert one day, just like her father!

2 ☆☆ **Circle the correct prepositions (1–6) in the biography.**

3 ☆☆ **Read the biography again and write the events in the box in the timeline below.**

met Alison ~~born~~ found a snake crocodile attack TV programmes

1978 1983 2003 2005 2012

1 born 3 ________ 5 ________

2 ________ 4 ________

4 ☆☆ **Match headings a–c with paragraphs 1–3.**

a Now ☐
b Early life ☐
c Main events ☐

Write a biography about a person who works with animals.

PLAN

5 ☆☆ **Think of a famous person who works with animals. Look for information on the internet and create a timeline about his or her life. Use Exercise 3 to help you.**

6 **Decide what information to include in each paragraph. Use Exercise 4 to help you.**

WRITE

7 ☆☆☆ **Write your biography. Remember to include three paragraphs, the past simple and time expressions and the *Useful language* expressions (see Student's Book, p89).**

CHECK

8 **Do you …**

- give information from the timeline of your famous person?
- do you write about the events in their life in the correct order?

7 REVIEW

VOCABULARY

1 Complete the crossword. Use the pictures.

ACROSS

4

6

10

13

14
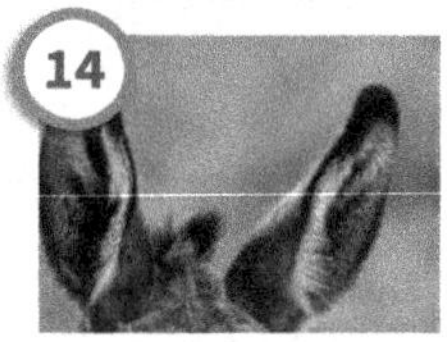

DOWN

1
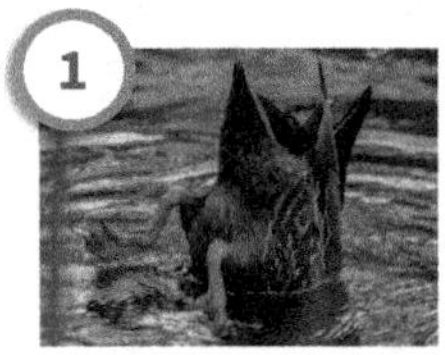
2

3
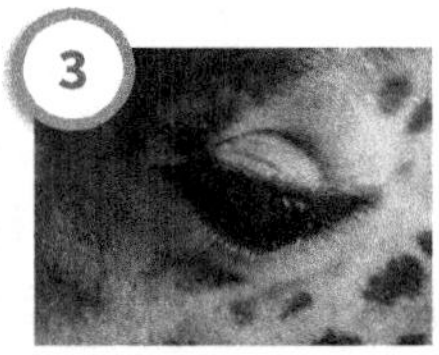
5

7
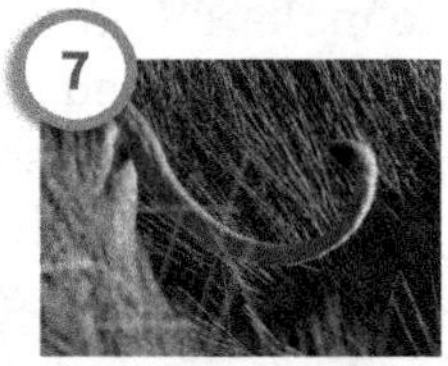
8

9

11

12
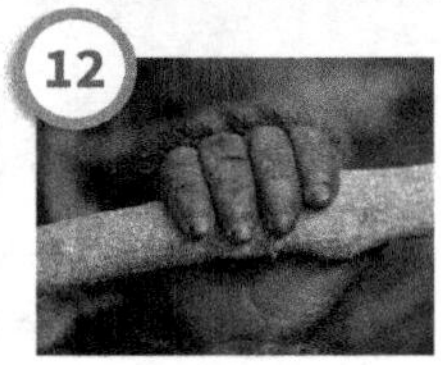

2 Complete the sentences with an adjective from the box.

lazy cute wild dangerous clever quiet beautiful heavy tiny large noisy

1 Kodiak brown bears are very ________ animals, but their babies are ________ – they are only about 23 centimetres long and they weigh only 450 gm.

2 Hippos are very ________ animals. They kill a lot of people.

3 My snake doesn't make much noise. He is very ________ .

4 When blue whales are born, they weigh about 2,700 kg. That's ________ !

5 Male lions are ________ . They sleep and the female lions hunt.

6 African grey parrots can learn 1,000 words. They are really ________ .

7 Howler monkeys are very ________ . You can hear them from 4km away!

8 Baby lions look ________, but be careful! They are ________ animals, not pets, and can attack you.

9 Oh, I love looking at photos of tigers! I think tigers are really ________ animals.

LANGUAGE IN ACTION

3 Circle the correct options in the dialogue.

A [1]*Was / Were* you at school yesterday?

B No, I [2]*wasn't / weren't.* [3]*There were / I was* on a school trip to an aquarium.

A [4]*Was it / Was there* good?

B Fantastic! There [5]*was / were* hundreds of different fish. My favourites [6]*were / was* the parrot fish and the clown fish. [7]*There was / It was* a dolphin area, too.

A [8]*Were there / There was* any sharks?

B Yes, [9]*they were / there were*, but there [10]*wasn't / weren't* time to go and see them. The aquarium's really big!

4 **Complete the text with the past simple form of the verbs in brackets.**

Last year I [1]________ (want) a pet, but I [2]________ (not have) any money so I [3]________ (go) to an animal rescue centre. At the centre I [4]________ (see) a lot of animals, but I [5]________ (not know) which one I [6]________ (like) best. Then I [7]________ (hear) a noise in a corner. A tiny white cat [8]________ (look) up at me with his big blue eyes. He was really cute. I [9]________ (take) him home, and he [10]________ (become) my best friend.

CUMULATIVE LANGUAGE

5 **Complete the conversation with the missing words. Circle the correct options.**

ISA Hi, Adela! How [1]________ your weekend?

ADELA [2]________ really nice, thanks! On Saturday morning I [3]________ basketball with my team – we [4]________ our match.

ISA No way! Your team always wins!

ADELA I know, but it [5]________ fun to play and we are still at the top of the league table. Anyway on Saturday afternoon I [6]________ to a football match with my cousins and my uncle – my team [7]________ so I [8]________ really happy!

ISA Wow! Lucky you!

ADELA Yes, then on Sunday afternoon, I [9]________ my friends and we went to the cinema. [10]________ a great film! The best bit was the burger we [11]________ in a restaurant near the cinema after the film. It was delicious!

ISA Really? Where's the restaurant?

ADELA On George Street. Let's go now!

	a	b	c
1	was	are	were
2	There was	There were	It was
3	plays	did play	played
4	lost	losed	loses
5	were	weren't	was
6	was	go	went
7	wins	won	win
8	wasn't	aren't	was
9	meet	meeted	met
10	It was	It weren't	It wasn't
11	eat	eated	ate

8 LOST AND FOUND

VOCABULARY

Places in town

1 ☆ **Look at the photos and complete the words for places.**

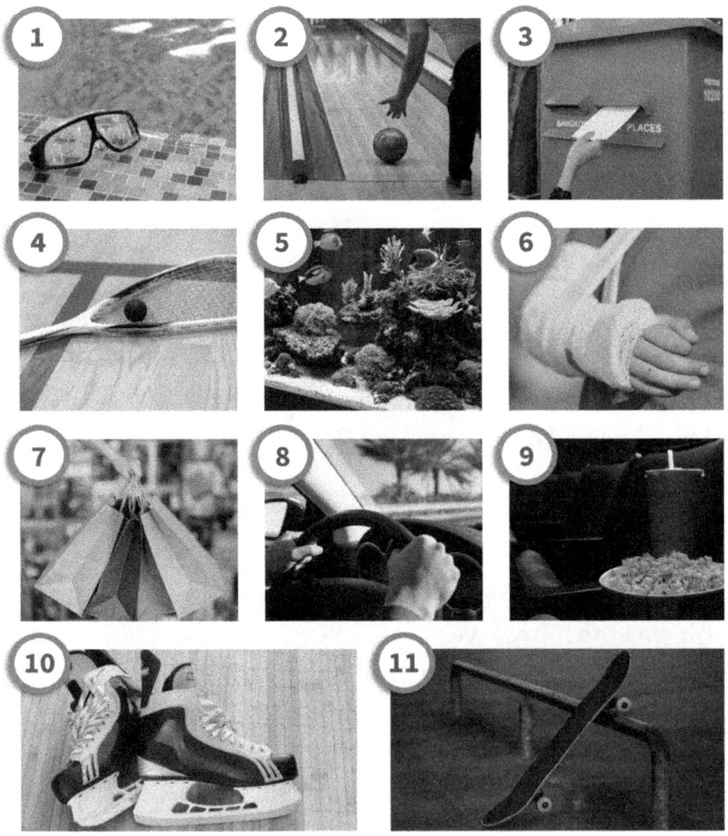

1 s w i m m i n g
p o o l

2 b _ _ _ _ _ _
a _ _ _ _

3 p _ _ _
o _ _ _ _ _

4 s _ _ _ _ _
c _ _ _ _ _

5 a _ _ _ _ _ _ _

6 h _ _ _ _ _ _ _

7 s _ _ _ _ _ _ _
c _ _ _ _ _

8 c _ _
p _ _ _

9 c _ _ _ _ _

10 i _ _ r _ _ _

11 s _ _ _ _
p _ _ _

2 ☆ **Look at the words in Exercise 1. How many are compound nouns?** ______

3 ☆ **Write a place from Exercise 1.**

1 I went there when I fell off my bike. hospital
2 It was cold in there but we wore gloves and it was fun! ______
3 We went there to buy some clothes and presents. ______
4 I went there to send a letter. ______

4 ☆☆ **Complete the text with the places from Exercise 1.**

My friend Edie lives in a small village. She always goes to the city to buy her clothes because there isn't a [1] shopping centre in her village. There's a library with lots of good books, and a [2] ______ to send letters, but nothing else. There isn't a [3] ______ to watch films!

I live in a big town and there's everything we need. I go to the [4] ______ to play tennis and take swimming classes at the [5] ______. In December, I love ice skating at the [6] ______ and going bowling at the [7] ______. My town has also got a [8] ______ – I was there last year when I broke my arm! But my favourite place is in the centre of town – it's an [9] ______ with lots of fish. My dad takes me there sometimes and leaves the car in a big [10] ______. After that, I usually go skateboarding in a cool [11] ______ nearby.

Explore it!

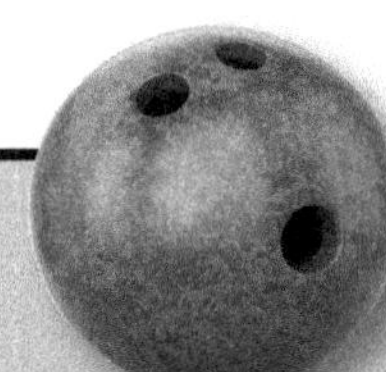

Guess the correct answer.

The first bowling alley opened in …

a London in 1889. b New York in 1840.

Find another interesting fact about a place from Exercise 1 in your country. Then send a question in an email to a classmate or ask them it in the next class.

READING

An online travel article

1 ★ **Look at the photos and read the article. Which photo (1–3) is the article not about?** ________

2 ★★ **Read the article and underline these words. Check their meaning in a dictionary and then complete the sentences.**

believe	belong	case	~~scuba diving~~	social media

1 I love swimming, but I prefer *scuba diving* underwater.

2 Matt's got a blog and shares his videos on ________ .

3 I can't ________ it! Our birthdays are on the same day!

4 Keep the camera safe. Put it in its ________ .

5 This cap isn't mine. Does it ________ to you?

3 ★★ **Read the article again. Put the events in the correct order (1–8).**

a Serina saw the photos on social media. ☐

b Serina went scuba diving. *1*

c The teacher put a message on social media. ☐

d The teacher looked at the photos on the camera. ☐

e Some schoolchildren found a camera on the beach. ☐

f Serina lost her camera. ☐

g The children and their teacher took the camera back to school. ☐

h Thousands of people shared the message. ☐

4 ★★★ **Imagine you are Serina. Write a 'Thank you' message to Mr Park Lee and his class. Write at least four sentences.**

Dear Mr Park Lee and students …

____

____

____

____

1

2

3

Lost under the sea

In March 2018, a class from Mount Elementary School in Su'ao, Taiwan, went to clean the beach. They found a camera in an underwater case. They didn't know it was a camera at first because the case had things from the sea all over it. They showed their teacher, Mr Park Lee. He opened the case. Inside was a digital camera, and no sea water!

The class took the camera back to school. Everyone had questions: Did it work? Were there any photos in it? Did it belong to someone from Su'ao? Could they find him or her? The camera worked! Mr Park Lee looked at the photos. They showed fish and people underwater, and streets in Japan. Mr Lee put some photos with a message in Chinese and Japanese on social media. He asked people to share the message with their friends. In the next 24 hours, thousands of people saw the message. One of them was Serina Tsubakihara, a Japanese student. She couldn't believe it – they were her photos!

Serina went scuba diving near Okinawa, in Japan, in September 2015. She lost her camera there. It was in the sea for more than two years and travelled 250 kilometres to Taiwan!

LANGUAGE IN ACTION

Past simple: questions

1 Match questions 1–5 with answers a–e.

1 Did Sami find his hat? c
2 Did the students go to the bowling alley? ☐
3 Did you and Dana finish your project? ☐
4 Did the ice rink close at six o'clock? ☐
5 Did Rosa go to the cinema? ☐

a Yes, we did.
b No, she didn't.
c Yes, he did.
d Yes, it did.
e No, they didn't.

2 Answer the questions for you. Tick (✓) the correct column.

Yesterday, did you …	Yes, I did.	No, I didn't.
… have a big breakfast?		
… do any sport?		
… go to the cinema?		
… visit a family member?		
… hang out with friends after school?		

3 Write the words in the correct order to make past simple questions.

1 Alex / to / post office / Did / go / the / ?
Did Alex go to the post office?
2 buy / a / Clara / bag / new / Did / ?
____
3 Did / time / they / good / have / a / ?
____
4 aquarium / the / Did / enjoy / you / ?
____
5 your / Did / to / parents / walk / town / ?
____

4 Write past simple questions. Do you know the answers?

1 Shakespeare / write *Romeo and Juliet* / ?
Did Shakespeare write Romeo and Juliet?
2 Marie Curie / win a Nobel Prize / ?
____
3 Picasso / paint the *Mona Lisa* / ?
____
4 Columbus / discover Australia / ?
____
5 Emma Watson / sing in the film *Frozen* / ?
____

5 Complete the conversation with past simple questions. Use the words in brackets and the <u>underlined</u> verbs.

MUM Hi, there! [1] Did you have a good match? (you / good match)
RAHEEM No, we <u>had</u> a terrible match.
MUM Oh, no! [2] _______________ ? (your team)
RAHEEM Yes. We <u>lost</u> 5–3.
MUM [3] _______________ ? (you / a goal)
RAHEEM No, I didn't <u>score</u> this time.
MUM What about Henrik? [4] _______________ ? (he)
RAHEEM No, he didn't <u>play</u>. He fell off his skateboard the other day.
MUM Oh, dear. [5] _______________ ? (he / anything)
RAHEEM Luckily he didn't <u>break</u> his leg. He just hurt it.
MUM Good! [6] _______________ after the match? (you / a snack)
RAHEEM Yes, I <u>had</u> some chocolate. That was the best part!

VOCABULARY AND LISTENING

Personal possessions

1 ☆ **Complete the definitions with the words in the box.**

bus pass camera ~~headphones~~ ID card keys money passport phone portable charger

We use …

1 _headphones_ to listen to music.
2 our ________ and ________ to show who we are.
3 ________ to buy things.
4 ________ to open a door.
5 a ________ to travel on public transport.
6 a ________ to text or talk to someone.
7 a ________ to take photos or make videos.
8 a ________ to keep our phone, tablet or laptop working.

2 ☆☆ **Complete the text with words from Exercise 1.**

ome News Blog Lifestyle

I had a bad day on Tuesday. I couldn't take the bus home because I couldn't find my [1] _bus pass_. Then I couldn't get into our flat because I didn't have my [2] ________. I used my [3] ________ to text my mum, but she was at the doctor's! I went to the library to do some homework on my laptop, but it had no battery and the [4] ________ was at home. I had some [5] ________ in my pocket, so I bought a drink at the café.

My sister loses things, too. Last July, she lost her [6] ________ on holiday and couldn't take any photos. Then she left her [7] ________ on a bus, so she couldn't listen to music on her phone. What a family!

A radio interview

8.01 **3** ☆ **Look at the photos and answer the questions with your own ideas. Then listen and check your answers.**

1 What did Sabina lose? ________
2 Where did she find it / them? ________

8.01 **4** ☆☆ **Listen again. Underline and correct one mistake in each sentence.**

1 The tickets <u>weren't</u> Sabina's birthday present.
were
2 Sabina asked her mum for help.
____
3 Sabina's friend put the envelope in the bin.
____
4 Sabina's CD wasn't in her room.
____
5 She didn't go to the concert. ________

8.01 **5** ☆☆ **Listen again and complete the sentences.**

1 The radio programme today is about ________.
2 Sabina's best friend never ________.
3 The questions helped Sabina ________.

LANGUAGE IN ACTION

Past simple: *Wh-* questions

1 ☆ Complete the questions with the question words in the box.

How much	What	When	~~Where~~	Who

1 A: *Where* did you buy your new headphones? B: Round the corner.
2 A: ________ did they cost? B: About €20.
3 A: ________ did you do last weekend? B: I went to the cinema.
4 A: ________ did you go with? B: My cousin.
5 A: ________ did you get that camera? B: Last week, for my birthday.

2 ☆☆ Write past simple questions. Then match them with answers a–e.

1 What / you / do / last night? [e]
What did you do last night?
2 How / you / get / to school / today? [ ]
____
3 Who / you / sit / with in class / yesterday? [ ]
____
4 Where / you / go / last weekend? [ ]
____
5 What time / get up / on Sunday? [ ]
____

a My best friend.
b Really late! At 11 o'clock!
c I caught the bus.
d I went to the aquarium with my friends.
e ~~I watched TV and read a book~~.

3 ☆☆☆ Complete the conversation with questions in the past simple. Use the answers to help you.

ANA Hey! I went to a baseball match in Chicago.
ROB Wow! When [1] *did you go* ?
ANA I went last weekend, on Saturday.
ROB Who [2] ________ ?
ANA I went with my family and my American cousin, Martin.
ROB Who [3] ________ ?
ANA I sat with Martin. He told me everything about the game.
ROB What [4] ________ ?
ANA I ate a big burger!
ROB How [5] ________ ?
ANA We went home by bus.
ROB What time [6] ________ ?
ANA I can't remember, but I know we got home really late!

4 ☆☆☆ Think about an interesting event you went to. Write the questions. Then answer them.

1 where / go? *Where did you go?*
2 when / go? ________
3 who / go with? ________
4 how / feel? ________

I went … ________
____
____
____

WRITING

A blog post

1 ★ **Read the blog post. What problem started Bruno's bad day? (Circle) the correct answer.**

a His camera didn't work.
b His sister's camera didn't work.
c His parents' car didn't work.

HOME | ABOUT ME | ARCHIVE | FOLLOW

BRUNO'S BIG BLOG

A bad day at the weekend

1 Last Saturday it was my sister's birthday. We gave her a camera, but it didn't work. My mum and dad decided to go to the shopping centre to change it, so we all got ready.

2 When we got into the car, it didn't work, so we decided to take the bus. But it got worse! It started raining so we arrived wet and cold at the shop. Tragic.

3 At the shop, the shop assistant asked for the receipt to change the camera, and guess what? My parents didn't have it … so my dad went back home to get it. After an hour, he came back and my sister got her new camera.

4 It was lunchtime, and we were really hungry, so we had lunch in the shopping centre. But when my parents wanted to pay, they couldn't find their wallets … they were at home!

5 When did you have a bad day at the weekend? What happened? Tell me!

2 ★★ **Read the blog again. Put the events in the correct order (1–5).**

a Bruno's dad went back home. ☐
b They needed a receipt for the camera. ☐
c They took the bus to the shopping centre. ☐
d The family car didn't work. 1
e Bruno's parents couldn't pay for lunch. ☐

3 ★★ **Join the sentences with *so*.**

1 It was my sister's birthday. We bought her a phone.
It was my sister's birthday, so we bought her a phone.
2 The phone didn't work. We decided to change it.
____
3 My dad showed the receipt. My sister got her new phone.
____
4 My parents couldn't find their wallets. They couldn't pay for lunch.
____

4 **Read the blog post again. Match topics a–e with paragraphs 1–5.**

a what happened next ☐
b what day it was and how it started ☐
c what happened later ☐
d sign off and ask questions ☐
e the end of the bad day ☐

Write a blog post about a bad day at the weekend.

PLAN

5 ★★ **Make notes about your bad day. Think about the answers to these questions.**

When did the bad day start?
What problems did you and your family / friends have?
When and where did each problem happen?
What did you do? What did the other people do?
How did you feel?

6 **Decide what information to include in each paragraph. Use the information in Exercise 4 to help you.**

WRITE

7 ★★★ **Write your blog post. Remember to include four paragraphs, the past simple for the questions at the end and the expressions from the *Useful language* box (see Student's Book, p101).**

CHECK

8 **Do you …**

- use a title for your blog post?
- use so to join ideas and explain the results?
- say how you felt on your bad day?

8 REVIEW

VOCABULARY

1 Where did Tim go last week? Match the sentences with the words in the box. There are four extra words.

aquarium   bowling alley   car park   cinema   hospital   ice rink   post office   shopping centre   skate park   sports centre   swimming pool

1 He posted a letter for his grandma. ____________
2 He watched a basketball match. ____________
3 He visited his sick uncle. ____________
4 He watched an amazing film. ____________
5 He bought a new pair of jeans. ____________
6 He saw lots of dolphins! ____________
7 He dived into the water. ____________

2 Which four places from Exercise 1 didn't Tim go to?

____________ ____________
____________ ____________

3 Complete the sentences with the words in the box.

camera   concert tickets   headphones   keys   money   passport   phone   tablet

1 I haven't got any ____________ to buy a drink.
2 You need your ____________ to travel to a different country.
3 These ____________ don't work. I can't hear anything!
4 These days, everyone's got a ____________ to text and call people.
5 It's easy to use a ____________. You just touch the screen and it works!
6 Let's buy ____________ to see Sia.
7 Héctor doesn't use his phone to take photos. He uses his ____________.
8 Where are the ____________ to open the door?

LANGUAGE IN ACTION

4 Complete the dialogue with the past simple questions and short answers. Use the verbs in brackets.

ARINA 1 ________ you ________ (go) to the bowling alley yesterday, Max?
MAX Yes, I 2 ________.
ARINA 3 ________ you ________ (meet) Olga there?
MAX No, I 4 ________. I was with Alex and Elena.
ARINA Cool! And 5 ________ you ________ (have) a good time?
MAX No, we 6 ________. Alex dropped the bowling ball on his foot!
ARINA Oh, dear! Poor Alex! 7 ________ his parents ________ (take) him to hospital?
MAX Yes, they 8 ________.
ARINA Was his foot OK? 9 ________ he ________ (break) it?
MAX No, he 10 ________. He was very lucky!

5 Write past simple questions.

1 What / you / do / last night? ______________________

2 How / your dad / get to work / this morning? ______________________

3 What time / you / arrive home / after school? ______________________

4 Who / you / see / yesterday? ______________________

5 Where / you / go / last weekend? ______________________

6 How / you / feel / after the exam? ______________________

CUMULATIVE LANGUAGE

6 Complete the conversation with the missing words. Circle the correct options.

BRENDA Hi, Theo. Where [1] __________ go yesterday?

THEO I [2] __________ to the ice rink to watch my brother.

BRENDA [3] __________ go ice skating, too?

THEO No! I don't [4] __________ ice skating. I think it's dangerous!

BRENDA Yes, me too! The first time I [5] __________ it I nearly [6] __________ my leg!

THEO The other problem is that [7] __________ usually a lot of people on the ice.

BRENDA Yes, you're right! [8] __________ does your brother go?

THEO He [9] __________ every week for about three hours. He says he wants to be the [10] __________ ice skater in town!

BRENDA [11] __________ you at the ice rink all day yesterday?

THEO Yes, but he [12] __________ me for dinner afterwards!

	a	b	c
1	do you	did you	you did
2	go	went	goes
3	Did you	You	Were you
4	like	likes	liked
5	try	tries	tried
6	broke	break	breaks
7	there is	there are	there were
8	How often	How many	How
9	practise	practises	practised
10	good	better	best
11	Did	Was	Were
12	take	took	takes

9 SUMMER FUN

VOCABULARY

Outdoor life

1 ★ **Look at the pictures. Complete the activities with the words and phrases in the box.**

a compass a fire a map a shelter fish ~~food and water~~ fruit over a campfire plants wood

1 find food and water

2 cook ______

3 pick ______

4 identify ______

5 light ______

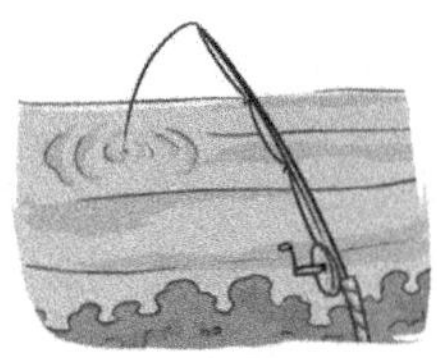

6 catch ______

7 collect ______

8 build ______

9 use ______

10 read ______

2 ★★ **Match the sentences with activities from Exercise 1.**

a You do this before nighttime. You sleep there. [8]
b You need to do this before you light a fire. [ ]
c You need to find trees with apples, pears, etc. to do this. [ ]
d You need to do this to see different places and where they are. [ ]
e You do this to know which way to go. [ ]
f You do this to keep warm and to cook. [ ]
g You do this when you are hungry or thirsty. [ ]

3 ★★ **Complete the text with the correct form of the verbs from Exercise 1.**

I often go to the mountains with my family. When we get there, some of us [1] collect wood for the fire and others [2] ______ a shelter. Next, we all go to [3] ______ water and [4] ______ fish for lunch. My dad always [5] ______ the fish over a campfire. It can take a long time to [6] ______ the fire if the wood is wet. In the afternoon, we go for a walk to [7] ______ plants. I write their names in my notebook. We sometimes [8] ______ fruit, too. We [9] ______ a compass in the mountains because it's easy to get lost!

4 ★★★ **Write about one or more outdoor activities that you do in the holidays. Look at Exercise 3 to help you.**

______

______

Explore it!

Guess the correct answer.

In this country, students have the longest school summer holidays in Europe. They get 13 weeks! Which country is it?

a Italy b Germany c Portugal

Find an interesting fact about how people spend their free time in your country. Then send a question in an email to a classmate or ask them it in the next class.

READING

A leaflet

ADVENTURE TRIPS

FIND AN ADVENTURE TRIP FOR YOU THIS SUMMER!

You'll learn new things and have lots of fun! Join us on one of our three Adventure Trips. Read and choose the best one for you!

1. WHITE WATER KAYAKING TRIP (THREE DAYS)

Day 1: Meet your instructors and practise on white water.

Day 2: Learn how to use a compass and choose the best part of the river for your kayak.

Day 3: Follow the fast water and show your instructors how good you are!

We'll also teach you to build a shelter and help you collect wood for a campfire.

2. MOUNTAIN CLIMBING TRIP (FIVE DAYS)

Days 1–2: Walk five kilometres in the mountains each day with your guide. Learn how to identify plants and pick the right fruit to eat!

Days 3–5: Spend three days mountain climbing. Learn how to read a map and help each other.

You won't get much time to sit down! But you'll become the best mountain climber!

3. WATER AND COUNTRYSIDE TRIP (SIX DAYS)

Day 1: Learn how to catch fish in the river and then cook them over a campfire!

Days 2–3: Travel along the river in a canoe and work as a team.

Days 4–6: Leave the water to go horse riding in the countryside with your guides!

You won't be bored on this trip. We'll play fun games and you'll make good friends!

WHAT ARE YOU WAITING FOR?

CHOOSE THE BEST ADVENTURE TRIP FOR YOU!

You'll learn new sports and skills, meet new people and have a great time!

For more information and booking details, visit our website.

We'll give you breakfast and lunch, but sometimes … you'll need to find your own dinner!

1 ★ **Read the leaflet. Then complete the sentences with the phrases in the box.**

White water kayaking   Mountain climbing   Water and countryside

1 You can learn how to read a map and identify plants on the ________ trip.

2 You can learn how to cook your own food over a campfire on the ________ trip.

3 You can learn how to use a compass on the ________ trip.

2 ★★ **Read the leaflet again and underline these words. Then check their meaning in a dictionary and complete the sentences.**

white water   ~~river~~   follow   guides   spend

1 There are lots of fish in that _river_.

2 The water in a river that moves very quickly is called ________.

3 Our mountain ________ showed us some good places to climb.

4 Don't walk alone in the forest. Always ________ the instructor.

5 I need to ________ more time learning how to build a shelter!

3 ★★★ **Answer the questions.**

1 On Trip 1, who do you meet on Day 1?

your instructors

2 On which day do you use a compass?

____

3 On Trip 2, how far do you walk on day one?

____

4 What things can you learn on Trip 2?

____

5 On Trip 3, when do you do water activities?

____

4 ★★★ **Answer the questions with your own ideas.**

1 Which trip is the most exciting? Why?

____

2 Which trip is the most difficult? Why?

____

LANGUAGE IN ACTION

Future with *will/won't*

1 ☆ **Circle the correct options.**

1 The climbing trip *be* / *will be* good fun. It *not will* / *won't* be boring.

2 We *won't* / *not will* make our own lunch. The instructors *make will* / *will make* it.

3 A: *Will you* / *You will* go on the kayaking trip?
B: Yes, *I'll* / *I will*.

4 A: *Will* / *Will not* the instructors make dinner for you?
B: No, they *not will* / *won't*.

2 ☆☆ **Write sentences with *I'll* or *I won't*.**

1 (✓) learn how to catch fish
I'll learn how to catch fish.

2 (✗) get bored
____

3 (✓) go in a canoe
____

4 (✗) stay for two weeks
____

5 (✓) walk six kilometres
____

6 (✓) cook food over a campfire
____

3 ☆☆ **Complete the email with the correct form of *will* and the verbs in brackets.**

Hi Victoria,

I got back a few hours ago from my family camping trip. It was OK, but my sister says she [1] won't go (not go) again. She also [2] ________ (not sleep) in a shelter again! She says she [3] ________ (go) with her friends on a beach holiday because it [4] ________ (be) sunny and they [5] ________ (not do) anything all day – just sleep and swim! She's 18 now, so I guess we [6] ________ (not be) together next summer. I [7] ________ (miss) her! How was your holiday?

4 ☆☆ **Write the words in the correct order to make questions. Then answer the questions for you in your notebook.**

1 with your family / Will / this year / you / go on holiday / ?
Will you go on holiday with your family this year?

2 you / Will / see / at the weekend / your best friend / ?
____

3 tomorrow / will / you / do / What / ?
____

4 this summer / go / you / Where / will / ?
____

5 will / you / Who / next week / see / ?
____

6 go shopping / you / Will / tomorrow / ?
____

5 ☆☆☆ **You are going on one of the adventure trips from the leaflet on p73. Make four predictions about it with *will/won't*.**

I'll make new friends.

1 ____________________

2 ____________________

3 ____________________

4 ____________________

VOCABULARY AND LISTENING

Holidays

1 ☆ **Complete the accommodation words in the spidergram with the missing vowels.**

HOLIDAYS

1 a p a rtm e nt
2 b _ d & br _ _ kf _ st
3 c _ mp _ r v _ n
4 c _ r _ v _ n
5 ch _ l _ t
6 c _ tt _ g _
7 h _ t _ l
8 t _ nt
9 y _ _ th h _ st _ l

2 ☆☆ **Complete the text with words from Exercise 1.**

My family and I want to go on holiday, but everyone wants to stay in a different place! My dad wants to stay in a [1]hotel ______, but my mum prefers a [2]b ______ & b ______. My brother loves moving from place to place, so he thinks a [3]c ______ v ______ is perfect! My grandma wants a little house like a [4]c ______, but my dad says that's very small. My aunt showed me a picture of an amazing city [5]a ______. It looks great, but I want to stay in a [6]y ______ h ______ – it's the best place to make friends!

A conversation

3 ☆ 9.01 **Listen to the conversation. Where will the girls spend their summer holidays? Circle the correct answer.**

a in a cottage b at home c in the USA

4 ☆☆ 9.01 **Listen again. Match the phrases with the people in the box.**

aunt and uncle	Camila	~~parents~~	Yana

1 on holiday in another country parents
2 really good fun ______
3 at home with her parents in the summer ______
4 invites her friend to do an outdoor activity ______

5 ☆☆ 9.01 **Listen again and answer the questions.**

1 How will Camila's parents travel around the USA?
in a camper van
2 Who will be with Camila for two weeks?
______
3 Whose parents have got a holiday cottage?
______
4 What will the parents of Camila's friend do in July and August?
______
5 Why does Camila ask her friend to stay with her?
______
6 Why doesn't Camila's friend like camping?
______

6 ☆☆☆ **Your parents are going on holiday and you will stay at home with someone else from your family. Make a spidergram with positive/negative things about this.**

LANGUAGE IN ACTION

Present continuous for future

1 ★ Match 1–6 with a–f.

1 My mum's working on Saturday. c
2 Are you watching the match tomorrow? ☐
3 Mario isn't playing tennis after school. ☐
4 Are your cousins arriving soon? ☐
5 We're going on a school trip tomorrow. ☐
6 How are you getting to the sports centre? ☐

a We're visiting a museum.
b My dad's driving me.
c ~~She's going to a meeting~~.
d He's going to the dentist.
e No, I'm not. I'm studying.
f Yes, they are. On Sunday.

2 ★★ Write sentences with the present continuous.

1 We / go / to the beach / at the weekend
We're going to the beach at the weekend.
2 Debra / not have / a birthday party / this year
____
3 My grandparents / fly / to Italy / in August
____
4 You / have / lunch / at a restaurant / on Sunday / ?
____
5 We / not do / anything special / this weekend
____
6 How / she / get / to work / today / ?
____

3 ★★ Complete the conversation with the present continuous form of the verbs in brackets.

CARLA What [1] *are you doing* (you / do) in the summer?
NICO In July I [2] ________ (go) to a summer camp in the mountains.
CARLA That sounds fun! [3] ________ (you / sleep) in a tent?
NICO No, I [4] ________ (not camp). We [5] ________ (stay) in chalets.
CARLA What [6] ________ (your parents / do)?
NICO They [7] ________ (start) their holidays in August. They [8] ________ (meet) me at the summer camp and we [9] ________ (drive) across the country in a camper van.

be going to

4 ★ Underline and correct one mistake in each sentence.

1 We going to visit the water park. *We're going*
2 Are you going see the new film? ________
3 I'm not go to buy a camera. ________
4 They're going living in the country. ________
5 Mia isn't to go swimming after school. ________
6 Leo going to learn to skateboard. ________

5 ★★★ Write questions with the present continuous or *be going to*. Then write answers for you.

1 What / do / this weekend? (present continuous)
What are you doing this weekend?
____
2 What / do / tonight? (present continuous)
____
____
3 What TV programmes / watch / this week? (be going to)
____
____
4 How / celebrate / your birthday / this year? (be going to)
____
____

WRITING

An email

1 ☆ **Read the email. How does Paige know Ava?**

____

2 ☆☆ **Circle the correct prepositions (1–10) in the email.**

Hi Ava,

1 Thanks for your email. I'm really excited you're coming to stay with us in New Zealand [1]*on* / *in* January! We'll have a great time! You'll enjoy Mission Bay and seeing our friends from primary school again.

2 Here are the arrangements. [2]*On* / *In* Friday, Mum and I are meeting you [3]*at* / *on* the airport in Auckland. Then we're going to have a night [4]*in* / *at* home and my dad's cooking. You're sleeping with me [5]*in* / *at* my room. We can talk about your new life in Australia and compare our schools!

3 [6]*In* / *On* Saturday, we're going to the beach. It'll be hot, so we'll go swimming. Hayley, Lily and Ryan from our primary class are coming, too! [7]*In* / *On* the evening, we're going to have dinner [8]*on* / *at* my favourite restaurant. Then [9]*on* / *at* Sunday, we're going to Te Urewera National Park for four days. We're staying [10]*in* / *on* a nice chalet. There are beautiful lakes and birds. What do you think?

4 It'll be great to see you again! Is there anything you would like to do? Let me know!

See you soon,

Paige xx

3 **Match topics a–d with paragraphs 1–4.**

a end the email ☐
b respond to your penfriend's last email ☐
c describe the first day ☐
d describe the weekend ☐

4 ☆☆ **Read the email again. Are the sentences *T* (true) or *F* (false)?**

1 Ava is travelling to Auckland by car. ___F___
2 Ava and Paige are sleeping in the same room. ______
3 They're spending one day at the beach. ______
4 They're having dinner at home on Saturday evening. ______
5 At Te Urewera National Park, they're not staying in a hotel. ______

Write an email to a friend from primary school about plans for their visit.

PLAN

5 ☆☆ **Your friend from primary school now lives in another place and is coming to stay with you. Make notes about these things for your email:**

your arrangements
things you intend to do
predictions about what will happen
the place where you are meeting them.

6 ☆☆ **Decide what information to include in each paragraph. Use the information in Exercise 3 to help you.**

WRITE

7 ☆☆☆ **Write your email. Remember to include four paragraphs, *will*, *going to* and the present continuous for future, and expressions from the *Useful language* box (see Student's Book, p113).**

CHECK

8 **Do you …**

- include an arrangement and a prediction for the weekend and the week ahead?
- make predictions about what will or won't happen?
- tell your penfriend where you are going to meet them?

9 REVIEW

VOCABULARY

1 Circle the correct verb.

1 *catch / build* a shelter
2 *light / cook* a fire
3 *build / pick* fruit
4 *catch / light* fish
5 *use / cook* over a campfire
6 *collect / build* wood
7 *read / collect* a map
8 *build / identify* plants

2 Find nine words for accommodation in the word search. Then match them with sentences 1–9 below.

C	T	E	N	T	Y	B	E	G	F	B
A	B	C	L	H	O	C	I	J	N	E
M	C	H	O	I	U	E	O	G	C	D
P	A	A	M	K	T	G	U	B	T	&
E	I	L	E	M	H	O	T	E	L	B
R	T	E	Y	R	H	M	E	V	L	R
V	F	T	X	C	O	T	T	A	G	E
A	K	C	Z	W	S	N	A	S	A	A
N	A	P	A	R	T	M	E	N	T	K
J	O	G	U	X	E	Q	M	R	B	F
K	P	E	W	O	L	T	X	S	C	A
M	R	V	C	A	R	A	V	A	N	S
O	U	H	O	H	I	R	A	Y	S	T

1 This can be a problem in the rain. ______
2 A place where young people normally stay. ______
3 You can drive with your bed in this! ______
4 A small country house. ______
5 You need a car to move this. ______
6 You only stay here to sleep and eat in the morning. ______
7 This is in a building, often in a city. ______
8 An expensive one has got five stars. ______
9 A small house usually made of wood. ______

LANGUAGE IN ACTION

3 Complete the conversation with the correct form of *will* or *won't*. Use the verbs in brackets.

Wall | Find friends | Chat

IAN 1h ago
1 ______ (we / sleep) in tents?

GUIDE 1h ago
No, you 2 ______ (not sleep) in a tent. You 3 ______ (stay) in a chalet. Every night, we 4 ______ (cook) dinner over a campfire.

IAN 1h ago
Sounds fun. What activities 5 ______ (we / do)?

GUIDE 1h ago
You 6 ______ (go) walking and climbing in the mountains. We 7 ______ (teach) you how to read a map so you 8 ______ (not get) lost. It 9 ______ (be) fantastic. You 10 ______ (not forget) the experience, I'm sure!

4 Complete the email with the present continuous form of the verbs in brackets.

Hi Sonia,

What 1 ______ (you / do) this summer? In July, my parents 2 ______ (work), so Pau and I 3 ______ (not / plan) anything special. He 4 ______ (go) to a football camp and I 5 ______ (stay) with my grandparents. Then in August we 6 ______ (fly) to Croatia for a family holiday. My parents 7 ______ (rent) an apartment at the beach, and then we 8 ______ (drive) up to the mountains in a camper van. I'm very excited!

5 Write sentences about the pictures. Use the correct form of *be going to* and the phrases in the box.

climb a mountain	get on a plane	go horse riding	play volleyball	sleep in a tent	walk in the forest

1 He ______________________

2 She ______________________

3 He ______________________

4 She ______________________

5 They ______________________

6 They ______________________

CUMULATIVE LANGUAGE

6 Complete the text with the missing words. Circle the correct options.

I had [1] ______________ amazing holiday of my life last year. [2] ______________ go? I went to Turkey on [3] ______________ adventure holiday! We built a shelter to sleep in and learned [4] ______________ new things, like how to catch fish and find fruit to eat in the forest. We did [5] ______________ sports, too. They were fun! I loved [6] ______________ kayaking but I [7] ______________ horse riding. It was frightening! I've got a lot of photos. Would you like to see [8] ______________?

This holiday was [9] ______________ than my holiday two years ago. Now I [10] ______________ lots of new friends. At the moment, we [11] ______________ emails to each other to get together this year. I can't [12] ______________!

	a	b	c
1	the more	most	the most
2	Where did I	What I did	When did I
3	some	a	an
4	much	a lot	a lot of
5	an	any	some
6	going	go	do
7	wasn't enjoy	didn't enjoy	not enjoy
8	them	they	it
9	better	the best	good
10	's got	got	've got
11	writing	're writing	write
12	to wait	wait	waiting

EXAM TIPS: Reading skills

Reading Part 2: Multiple matching

In this part of the test you have to read three short texts about three different people. They are all about the same topic. The title tells you what the topic is. There are seven questions. They all start with: *Which person ...?* The answer to each question is the name of one of the three people. To answer the question you need to circle the correct answer, A, B or C.

Example:

	Tim	*Tom*	*Ted*
Which person did a lot of sport at school?	*A*	*B*	*C*

Exam guide: Multiple matching

- Start by reading the title of the text so you know what the topic is.
- Read all the questions carefully and underline the important words. This helps when you look for the same information in the texts.

  Example:

  Which person did a lot of sport at school?
- Now read the three texts for the first time without stopping. Maybe you see information similar to the questions, but read to the end.
- Now read the first question again. Then look at the texts to find which person says this. Maybe you remember something from one of the texts, so go to that text first to check. If not, just read from the beginning until you find what you need.
- When you find the correct answer, underline the words in the text with the same meaning as the question. Write the number of the question next to the part you underlined. Then circle your answer, A, B or C.

  Example:

  When I was a teenager I was in the school hockey, athletics and swimming teams.
- Then read the next question and do the same until you finish.
- You don't lose points for a wrong answer, so always circle a letter, even if you're not sure.

REMEMBER!

When you look for the answer, remember that the words in the question are probably different from the words in the text, but the meaning is the same. So if you see a word in the text that is the same as a word in the question, it is not automatically the correct answer.

Example:

I did a lot of sport after school when I was younger.

This is **NOT** the correct answer to the example question, because the meaning is different from the question.

Reading Part 2 practice: Multiple matching

1 Underline the most important words in these questions.

0 Which person does <u>a lot of sport</u> at the <u>weekend</u>?

Which person

1 loves trying new activities after school?
2 has got a lot of online friends?
3 reads science and nature magazines on the internet?
4 wants to study art or drama at school next year?
5 hasn't got any aunts, uncles or cousins?
6 doesn't like living in a big city?

Tip! Underlining the most important words in the questions helps you to remember the information you need to find in the text.

2 Match words 1–9 with their opposites in the box.

after	boring	difficult	evening	finish	good	hate	late	short	~~small~~

0 big small

1 easy ______
2 early ______
3 love ______
4 long ______
5 start ______
6 before ______
7 morning ______
8 fun ______
9 bad ______

Tip! When reading the text, look for words or phrases which are opposites (often with a negative verb) or synonyms of the words in the question.

3 Read the text and match the words in bold with the synonyms 1–9.

One place in my **road** that's very popular with **young people** is the skate park. Some of my friends spend all their **leisure time** there. There is also a **big** sports centre near me, with some good **courses**, like swimming and dancing. **Many** of my friends **tell me** they would like to go there too, but the **price** is too high. I **travel** to a cheaper gym but it's not very near my house and so it's **difficult** to get to.

0 street road
1 a lot ______
2 large ______
3 say ______
4 free time ______
5 teenagers ______
6 hard ______
7 go ______
8 cost ______
9 classes ______

4 Choose the option, A or B, which has the same meaning as the question.

0 Which person has a lot of homework to do?
(A) I spend about two hours every night on school work.
B In my school the teachers don't usually give us much homework.

1 Which person isn't happy about their hair colour?
A I've got red hair but I don't mind. It's the same as Ed Sheeran's!
B Everyone in my family has got blonde hair. It's boring. I want to be different.

2 Which person reads information about science on the internet?
A There is so much interesting stuff to read online these days, especially science articles.
B I love reading my dad's science magazines. He buys them every month.

3 Which person doesn't mind getting up early in the morning?
A I have to get up at seven so I'm not late for school, but that isn't a problem.
B I'm glad when it's Saturday and I can get up late.

4 Which person thinks living in the country is boring?
A People say that the country is boring but I think there's lots to do.
B I'm happy I live in the city. I'm sure it's more exciting than being in a village.

EXAM TIPS: Writing skills

Writing Part 6: Writing a short email or note

In this part of the test, you have to write a short email or note of 25 words or more. Under the instructions there is a space to write the text.

The instructions in the test tell you exactly what you need to do.

Example:

*You want to **go to the cinema** with **your friend** Jan on **Saturday**. Write an email to Jan.*

The instructions also explain three things you need to include in the text. For example:

In the email:

- **ask** Jan to **go to the cinema** with you
- say **what film** you want to see
- say **where** you can **meet**.

Exam guide: Writing a short email or note

- It is important to include all the points from the instructions in the text. It is also better to keep them in the same order as in the instructions.
- The text needs
  - an opening sentence
  - three sentences, one for each point
  - a sentence to close (for example a question asking your friend's opinion)
  - (in an email) your name at the end.
- When you finish, read the text again and count the number of words. If you have included all the information from the plan above, the text should be at least 25 words. If it's more, that's OK. If you haven't written 25 words, go back and check that you have included all the points and the opening and the closing sentences.

Writing Part 7: Writing a short story

In this part of the test, you have to write a short story of 35 words or more. To help you there are three pictures. You write the story they show. Under the pictures there is a space to write your story.

Exam guide: Writing a short story

- Don't start writing immediately. Look at the pictures for a minute and decide what the story is about. A good way to plan a story is to think about *Who? Where? When?* and *What?*
- Give any people in the picture a name. Then write any useful vocabulary you want to use (nouns, verbs, adjectives, etc.) next to each picture.
- Decide how to start (e.g. *One day/Yesterday*). Use the past tense when you write your story.
- When you finish writing, count the words. You need to write at least 35 words.

REMEMBER!

You will be given a piece of paper to make notes. Use it to plan your writing.

Writing Parts 6 & 7 practice: An email or note; a short story

1 Match the phrases from a text message with the right category A–C.

> **Tip!** For this part of the test, try to use different phrases for inviting and suggesting ideas.

A opening B inviting or suggesting C closing phrase

0 *I'd like to see the new X-men film.* B

1 What do you think? ____

2 Do you want to go swimming this afternoon? ____

3 Let me know soon. ____

4 Hey ____

5 Shall we meet at the bus stop at seven? ____

6 Hi Jan ____

7 We can try the new pool. ____

8 How about going to the cinema on Saturday? ____

2 Order the words to make sentences from an email.

0 *cheap / to / a / go / restaurant / Let's / .* Let's go to a cheap restaurant.

1 want / in / Do / holidays / to / you / meet / the / ?

______

2 for / Why / days / we / don't / go / a few / camping / ?

______

3 what / know / Let / you / me / think / .

______

4 Tania / Hi / ,

______

5 climbing / I'd / go / again / to / like / .

______

6 my / can / tent / take / We / brother's / .

______

3 Separate the text into words and sentences. Then rewrite the email with the correct format and punctuation in your notebook.

> **Tip!** Always check your writing for spelling or punctuation.

heyjosedoyouwanttohangouttogetheronsaturdaywecangotothe newshoppingcentreshallicometoyourhouseatfourletmeknowsoonpepe

Hey Jose,

4 Correct the spelling of these words.

0 *swiming* swimming

1 shoping ______

2 wich ______

3 tenis ______

4 Wenesday ______

5 tomorow ______

6 bycicle ______

7 diferent ______

8 scool ______

9 begining ______

5 Put the words in the box in the correct place in the story.

> **Tip!** Use time words like *yesterday*, *after* or *then* to make the order of events clear. Use words like *but* and *so* to show how the events connect.

After but so Then ~~Yesterday~~

[0] Yesterday Annie had a technology presentation at school, [1] ______ she got up late. [2] ______ she got to school, she saw her notes weren't in her bag. They were important, [3] ______ she phoned her dad and asked him to look for them. He found them in her room. [4] ______ he brought her notes to school. She was very happy.

EXAM TIPS: Listening skills

Listening Part 4: Three-option multiple choice

In this part of the test you listen to five short texts. You always hear the text twice. Each text is about something different, and the question usually explains who is speaking, who they are speaking to and what they are talking about.

Example:

You will hear ***two friends*** *talking about* ***their plans for the weekend.***

You then have to answer a question about each text, with three options, A, B and C.

Example:

You will hear two friends talking about their plans for the weekend. ***What do they both plan to do?***

A They are ***both going*** *to a* ***basketball match.***

B They are ***both visiting*** *their* ***grandparents.***

C They are ***both going shopping*** *with* ***friends.***

You can write your answers on the question paper. At the end of the test, you will have six minutes to put all your answers on a separate answer sheet.

Exam guide: Three-option multiple choice

- You have time before you listen to read the questions. Read them carefully because they tell you what you need to listen for.
- Underline the important words in the question. In the example the most important word in the question is **both**.

  Example:

  A They are both going to a basketball match.

  B They are both visiting their grandparents.

  C They are both going shopping with friends.
- When you listen the first time, try and decide what the correct answer is and circle A, B or C. If you're not sure, don't worry. The second time you listen you can check your first answer or decide for the first time.
- Sometimes the first time you listen you hear that one answer is definitely wrong. Cross it out. Then the second time you listen, just focus on the other two possible answers.
- Always give an answer, even if you don't know which one is correct. You don't lose points for a wrong answer.
- When you have heard one text twice, don't spend a lot of time thinking about it. Focus on the next listening text when it starts.

REMEMBER!

You will usually hear the people talk about all the possible answers in some way but this is a 'trap'. Only one answer is correct.

To avoid 'traps', listen carefully to every word. You will hear negative verbs (for example: *I'm not visiting my grandparents this weekend*) or things which are similar but not the same as the correct answer (for example: *I'm going shopping with my sister on Saturday*).

Listening Part 4 practice: Three-option multiple choice

E.01 **1 Listen to the sentences. Write *Y* (yes) if they are positive or *N* (no) if they are negative.**

1 ______ 2 ______ 3 ______ 4 ______ 5 ______ 6 ______

E.02 **2 Is the meaning of the sentences you hear the same as sentences 1–6? Write *Y* (yes) or *N* (no).**

1 I decided not to buy the shirt because I didn't like the colour. ______
2 It takes Martin a quarter of an hour to walk home. ______
3 It was sunny yesterday. ______
4 Martin is flying to Spain on holiday. ______
5 Paula's sister has got dark hair. ______
6 The teacher tells Eric to do his homework again. ______

E.03 **3 Read sentences 1–6. Then listen and correct the information that is different.**

1 Alex went to Scotland by coach last year. ______________
2 Laia is going to stay in a hotel with her grandparents. ______________
3 Donna usually goes to the bowling alley at the weekend. ______________
4 Harry lost his bus pass yesterday. ______________
5 Last week Megan saw a programme about bears on TV. ______________
6 Tom has got a basketball match on Saturday morning. ______________

E.04 **4 Listen and choose the correct option, A or B. You will hear each text twice.**

1 The teacher has got a problem with Sarah's homework because
   A she made a lot of mistakes.
   B she did the wrong page.
2 What's the weather like today?
   A It's cold and wet.
   B It's cloudy and warm.
3 What did Corrin and Vanessa do today?
   A They went out for a meal.
   B They went out with school friends.
4 How did Nico get home after the concert?
   A He caught the last bus.
   B His friend's dad gave him a lift.
5 What did Ollie buy at the shopping centre?
   A a new sports bag
   B some new joggers
6 What does Chloe's mother want her to do?
   A go shopping
   B tidy her room

Present continuous: affirmative and negative

Affirmative		Negative	
I'm	eating dinner.	I'm not	eating dinner.
You're		You're not	
He's / She's / It's		He's / She's / It's not	
We're		We're not	
You're		You're not	
They're		They're not	

- We use the present continuous to talk about actions in progress at the time of speaking.
  You are reading this sentence.
- For the affirmative, we use **subject** + ***be*** + **verb** + ***-ing***.
  The dog is sleeping. *The children are playing.*
- For the negative, we put ***not*** after ***be***.
  She is not (isn't) downloading songs.

Present continuous: questions

(Question word)	*be*	Subject	Verb + *ing*
-	Am	I	reading?
-	Are	you	thinking?
-	Is	he / she / it	sleeping?
-	Are	we / you / they	learning?
What	are	you	doing?
Where	is	she	going?

Short answer	
Affirmative	**Negative**
Yes, I am.	No, I'm not.
Yes, you are.	No, you aren't.
Yes, he / she / it is.	No, he / she / it isn't.
Yes, we / you / they are.	No, we / you / they aren't.

- To form questions, we use ***be*** + **subject** + **verb** + ***-ing***.
  Are you listening?
- We don't use the **verb** + ***-ing*** in short answers.
  Yes, I am. (NOT *Yes, I am ~~listening~~.*)
- We form information questions with the ***Wh-*** question word before *be*.
  Who are you talking to? *What are they doing?*

Spelling: *-ing* form

- With most verbs, we add ***-ing*** to the infinitive.
  eat – eating *read – reading* *think – thinking*
- For verbs ending in ***-e***, we remove the ***-e*** and add ***-ing***.
  write – writing *have – having* *give – giving*
- For verbs ending in a vowel and a consonant, we double the final consonant and add ***-ing***.
  stop – stopping *shop – shopping*
  plan – planning

Present simple and present continuous

- We use the present simple to talk about facts, habits and routines.
  Red and yellow make orange.
  I read a lot of books.
  He usually wears boots.
- We use the present continuous to talk about actions in progress at the time of speaking.
  I read a lot of books. At the moment, I'm reading a really good one.
  He usually wears boots, but he's wearing trainers today.
- Some verbs are not usually used in the continuous form: ***hate***, ***know***, ***like***, ***love***, ***need***, ***remember***, ***think***, ***understand***, ***want***.
  I like that song. (NOT *I'm ~~liking~~ that song.*)
- We use expressions like ***at the moment*** and ***right now*** with the present continuous.
  He's playing video games at the moment.

LANGUAGE PRACTICE

UNIT 5

Present continuous: affirmative and negative

1 **Write the *-ing* form of the verbs.**

1 eat ___eating___
2 write ______
3 chat ______
4 play ______
5 swim ______
6 have ______

2 **Complete the sentences with the present continuous form of the verbs in the box.**

chat	get dressed	have	listen	~~read~~	use

1 Luis ___is reading___ a book.
2 My grandparents ______ their dinner.
3 The teacher ______ to our stories.
4 My mum ______ to go to a party this evening.
5 You ______ my computer and I need it!
6 I ______ to my friends online.

3 **Rewrite the sentences in Exercise 2 in the negative form of the present continuous. Use contractions.**

1 Luis isn't reading a book.
2 ______
3 ______
4 ______
5 ______
6 ______

Present continuous: questions

4 **Complete the questions with the present continuous form of the verbs in brackets. Then write the short answers.**

1 ___Are___ you ___doing___ (do) your homework?
Yes, ___I am.___
2 ______ your sister ______ (read) a book?
No, ______
3 ______ your uncle ______ (make) dinner?
Yes, ______
4 ______ we ______ (have) sandwiches for lunch?
No, ______
5 ______ my grandparents ______ (watch) TV?
No, ______
6 ______ the cat ______ (sleep) on my bed?
Yes, ______

Present simple and present continuous

5 **Complete the rules. Write *present continuous* or *present simple*.**

1 To talk about facts, routines and habits, we use the ______.
2 To talk about an action in progress at the time of speaking, we use the ______.
3 We use *always*, *often*, *usually*, *sometimes* and *never* with the ______.
4 We use *right now* and *at the moment* with the ______.

6 **Circle the correct options.**

My name is Carolina. At the moment, I'm on holiday and I [1]*help* / *'m helping* my dad. We have a big garden and he usually [2]*works* / *is working* all the time, so he's tired at the weekend. Now he is on holiday, too. I [3]*like* / *'m liking* flowers, and we usually [4]*collect* / *are collecting* some to put in the house. Right now my dad [5]*paints* / *is painting* the garden wall and, of course, my brother [6]*watches* / *is watching* us do all the work!

LANGUAGE REFERENCE

Comparatives

Comparatives	
Short adjectives *smart*	add *-**er***: *smarter*
Short adjectives ending in vowel + consonant *big*	double the final consonant and add *-**er***: *bigger*
Adjectives ending in *-e* *safe*	add *-**r***: *safer*
Adjectives ending in *-y* *easy*	remove the *-**y*** and add *-**ier***: *easier*
Long adjectives *interesting*	put ***more*** before the adjective: *more interesting*
Irregular adjectives *good* *bad*	 *better* *worse*

- We use comparative adjectives to compare one thing with another. We use the verb ***be*** + **a comparative adjective** + ***than***.
  José is taller than his father.

Superlatives

Superlatives	
Short adjectives *smart*	add *-**est*** *smartest*
Short adjectives ending in vowel + consonant *big*	double the final consonant and add *-**est***: *biggest*
Adjectives ending in *-e* *safe*	add *-**est***: *safest*
Adjectives ending in *-y* *easy*	remove the *-**y*** and add *-**iest***: *easiest*
Long adjectives *interesting*	put ***most*** before the adjective: *most interesting*
Irregular adjectives *good* *bad*	 *best* *worst*

- We use superlative adjectives to say a thing or person has got the most of a particular quality. We use ***the*** with a **superlative adjective**.
  José is the tallest person in his family.

Comparatives

1 Match the adjectives with their opposites.

1 big [d] a unhealthy
2 boring [ ] b short
3 easy [ ] c new
4 tall [ ] ~~d small~~
5 old [ ] e difficult
6 healthy [ ] f interesting

2 Write the comparative form of the adjectives in the box next to the comparative with the same spelling rule.

bad comfortable heavy nice ~~old~~ thin

1 smarter older
2 bigger ______
3 safer ______
4 easier ______
5 more interesting ______
6 better ______

3 Write sentences with comparatives about Zehra's family.

1 My sister / short / me
My sister is shorter than me.
2 My brother / young / me
______
3 My sister / funny / my brother
______
4 My mum / thin / my dad
______
5 My brother / old / my sister
______
6 My / cousin / intelligent / me
______

Superlatives

4 Complete the table with the superlative.

Adjective	Comparative	Superlative
high	higher	1 the highest
amazing	more amazing	2 ______
easy	easier	3 ______
bad	worse	4 ______
popular	more popular	5 ______
big	bigger	6 ______

5 Complete the sentences with the superlative form of the adjectives in brackets.

1 I think my dad is the best (good) dad in the world.
2 Many footballers are the ______ (rich) people in sport.
3 My mum says Formula 1 racing is the ______ (fast) sport.
4 This is the ______ (heavy) bag in the world! What have you got in it?
5 I think ice hockey is one of the ______ (dangerous) sports.
6 Which is the ______ (easy) sport to learn?

6 Complete the text with the comparative or superlative form of the adjectives in brackets.

On Saturdays I usually go and see my cousin play football. She's 1 the best (good) player in the team. She always scores 2 ______ (amazing) goals! She's 3 ______ (tall) player in the team and she's 4 ______ (fast) than the others. I think she's also 5 ______ (intelligent) than her team mates because she watches what is happening all the time! She's also 6 ______ (popular) player in the team!

LANGUAGE REFERENCE

UNIT 7

was/were

Affirmative		Negative	
I / He / She / It	was good.	I / He / She / It	wasn't good.
You / We / They	were good.	You / We / They	weren't good.

Question	Short answer	
	Affirmative	Negative
Was I / he / she / it good?	Yes, I / he / she / it was.	No, I / he / she / it wasn't.
Were you / we / they good?	Yes, you / we / they were.	No, you / we / they weren't.

- ***Was*** and ***were*** are the past simple forms of ***be***.
  There was a special gorilla in Barcelona zoo.
  The elephants were born without tusks.
- To form questions, we use ***was/were***. We don't use ***do***.
  Was he a white tiger? (NOT ~~*Does he was a white tiger*~~?)
  Were the elephants enormous?
- We form information questions with the ***Wh-*** question before ***was/were***.
  What was it? *Where were you last night?*

there was/were

	Affirmative	Negative
Singular	There was a gorilla at the zoo.	There wasn't a gorilla at the zoo.
Plural	There were three lions.	There weren't three lions.

Question	Short answer	
	Affirmative	Negative
Was there a gorilla at the zoo?	Yes, there was.	No, there wasn't.
Were there three lions?	Yes, there were.	No, there weren't.

- ***There was/were*** are the past simple forms of ***there is/are***.
  There was a park here. *There were two cars.*
- We use ***there was*** with singular countable nouns and uncountable nouns.
  There was a pen here. *There was some milk in the fridge.*
- We use ***there were*** with plural countable nouns.
  There were a lot of tourists in our town last weekend.
- In questions and negatives, we usually use ***any*** with plural countable and uncountable nouns
  Were there any interesting animals at the zoo?
  Was there any bread at home?
  There weren't any cats. *There wasn't any rice.*

Past simple: regular and irregular verbs

- We use the past simple to talk about completed events and actions in the past.
  I played basketball yesterday.
  He lived in London last year.

Spelling

most verbs	add ***-ed:*** *show – showed*
verbs ending in *-e*	add ***-d:*** *live – lived*
verbs ending in **consonant + *-y***	remove the *-y* and add ***-ied:*** *study – studied*
verbs ending in **consonant + vowel + consonant**	double the final consonant and add ***-ed:*** *shop – shopped* *stop – stopped*

Irregular verbs

- Irregular past simple verbs don't follow any pattern.
  get – got *do – did* *see – saw* *have – had*

Past simple: negative

	didn't	Infinitive	Other words
I / You / He / She / It / You / We / They	didn't	play	football yesterday.
		go	to the cinema.

- To form the past simple negative, we use **subject + *didn't* + infinitive** without ***to***.
  Javier didn't watch TV last night.
  They didn't have lunch at home today.
- We can use time expressions such as ***yesterday***, ***last night***, ***last weekend*** and ***last summer*** with the past simple. We usually put them at the end of a sentence.
  We went to a safari park last weekend.
- We use ***ago*** with the past simple to talk about when something happened. We usually put it at the end of a sentence.
  Alex arrived home two hours ago.

was/were

1 Circle the correct options.

1 The monkey (was) / *were* in a tree at the zoo.
2 The baby elephant *was* / *were* beautiful!
3 The bears *wasn't* / *weren't* very big, but the lions *was* / *were* enormous!
4 It *wasn't* / *weren't* a very interesting documentary – it *was* / *were* very boring!
5 We *was* / *were* at the zoo for hours!
6 Diego *was* / *were* happy but Maria *wasn't* / *weren't*!

2 Put the words in the correct order to make questions. Then complete the answers with *was* or *were*.

1 happy / Maria / was / ?
A: Was Maria happy?
B: Yes, she was.
2 yesterday / were / Where / you / ?
A: ______
B: I ______ at home.
3 were / Who / with / you / ?
A: ______
B: My friend ______ at home with me.
4 the / zoo / Was / big / ?
A: ______
B: Yes, it ______ enormous!
5 most / What / animal / was / the / interesting / ?
A: ______
B: The tigers! They ______ beautiful.

there was/were

3 Circle the correct options.

For many years [1]*there wasn't* / (*there weren't*) many people in my town and [2]*there wasn't* / *there weren't* a place to see animals, but in 2015 everything changed – [3]*there was* / *there were* houses, people, children, shops and [4]*there was* / *there were* a new animal park! [5]*There wasn't* / *There weren't* any big animals, like elephants, but [6]*there was* / *there were* lovely little animals, like rabbits and lots of different birds. Now, it's my favourite place!

Past simple: regular and irregular verbs

4 Write the past simple form of the verbs in the table

Regular	watch	live	hate
	1 watched	2 ______	3 ______
	plan	stop	study
	4 ______	5 ______	6 ______
Irregular	do	eat	get
	7 ______	8 ______	9 ______
	go	have	see
	10 ______	11 ______	12 ______

5 Complete the text with the past simple form of the verbs in brackets.

We [1] arrived (arrive) at the animal park in the morning. My little sister [2]______ (want) to see the birds, but they were at the other end of the park. She [3]______ (cry) for a few minutes, then I [4]______ (show) her the rabbits. She [5]______ (love) them! She [6]______ (play) with them for hours!

6 Write the words in the correct order to make sentences.

1 week / my / went / to / dad / mountains / Last / I / the / with
Last week I went to the mountains with my dad.
2 brown / bears / saw / big / We / two
______
3 so / we / had / My / dad / a sandwich / was / hungry
______
4 behind / I / bear / me / heard / a
______
5 up / a / tree / I / went / bear / ate / my / sandwich / and / the
______
6 My / the / ran / to / car / eat / his / sandwich, but / dad / didn't
______

LANGUAGE REFERENCE

Past simple: questions

did	Subject	Infinitive	Short answer	
			Affirmative	Negative
Did	I / you / he / she / it / we / you / they	play?	Yes, I / you / he / she / it / we / you / they did.	No, I / you / he / she / it / we / you / they didn't.

- We make past simple questions with ***did*** + **subject** + **the infinitive**.
  Did she enjoy the yoga class?

Past simple: *Wh-* questions

Question word	*did*	Subject	Infinitive
Who	did	I / you / he / she / it / we / you / they	go with?
What time			go?
Where			go?
What			go for?
When			go?
How			go?

- We form *Wh-* questions in the past simple with a **question word** + ***did*** + **subject** + **the infinitive.**
  What time did you go to bed?
  Where did they go on holiday?
  What did you do at the weekend?
  Who did she see there?
  How did he feel?
  When did you arrive?

Past simple: questions

1 Match questions 1–5 with answers a–e.

1 Did you go to the post office this morning? [d]
2 Did you and Antonia watch TV last night? [ ]
3 Did the shop close early yesterday? [ ]
4 Did your friends go to the bowling alley with you? [ ]
5 Did our English teacher correct our homework? [ ]

a No, she didn't.
b Yes, we did.
c Yes, they did.
d ~~Yes, I did~~.
e No, it didn't.

2 Look at the information about the activities Sergio and Andrea did at the weekend. Write short answers.

	Go bowling	Tidy bedroom	Visit grandparents	Go swimming
Sergio	✓	✗	✓	✗
Andrea	✗	✓	✓	✗

1 Did Sergio go bowling? Yes, he did.
2 Did Sergio tidy his bedroom? ______
3 Did Andrea tidy her bedroom? ______
4 Did Sergio visit his grandparents? ______
5 Did Andrea go swimming? ______
6 Did Sergio go swimming? ______

3 Write questions and short answers.

1 your cousins / see / the fish / at the / aquarium ✓
A: Did your cousins see the fish at the aquarium?
B: Yes, they did.

2 Daniel / go to / the skate park / yesterday ✗
A: ______
B: ______

3 you and Melody / meet / at the cinema / today ✓
A: ______
B: ______

4 Olga / do / judo / last year ✗
A: ______
B: ______

5 you / stay / at the hospital / for a long time ✓
A: ______
B: ______

Past simple: *Wh-* questions

4 Circle the correct options.

1 **A:** *What* / *Where* did you do at the weekend?
B: I stayed at home.

2 **A:** *Where* / *When* did they play handball on Sunday?
B: In the sports centre.

3 **A:** *What* / *Who* did he see at the ice rink?
B: Nobody he knew.

4 **A:** *How* / *When* did he feel?
B: Not very well.

5 **A:** *How* / *What* time did they leave?
B: About 5 pm.

6 **A:** *When* / *Who* did they catch the train?
B: Early this morning.

5 Complete the dialogue with *Wh-* question words from Exercise 4.

Yusaf: I like your phone. [1] Where did you get it?
Ali: In the new shopping centre.
Yusaf: Was it expensive?
Ali: I don't know! It was a present.
Yusaf: [2] ______ bought it for you?
Ali: My mum. She got it for my birthday!
Yusaf: Wow, that's a fantastic present! [3] ______ did she get it?
Ali: She got it last week when we went shopping, but I didn't see her buy it!
Yusaf: [4] ______ did you feel when you got it?
Ali: Surprised and happy!
Yusaf: [5] ______ did I get you? I can't remember!
Ali: Nothing, you forgot!
Yusaf: Sorry!

Future with *will/won't*

Affirmative		Negative		Question		Short answer	
						Affirmative	Negative
I/You/He/ She/It/We / You/They	will pass the exam.	I/You/He/ She/It/We / You/They	won't pass the exam.	Will I/you/ he/she/it/ we/you/they	pass the exam?	Yes, I/you/ he/she/it/ we/you/they will.	No, I/you/ he/she/it/ we/you/they won't.

- We use ***will*** and ***won't*** to make predictions about the future.
  Computers will control our lives in the future.
- ***Will/Won't*** doesn't change in the third person.
- We change the word order when we form questions. We don't use ***do/does***.
  Will we travel in cars in the future?
- In informal English we use the contraction ***'ll***.
  They'll sleep in a camper van on holiday.

Present continuous for future

- We can use the present continuous to talk about fixed arrangements in the future.
  I'm meeting my friend Maite at 6.30.
  My sister's travelling to Brazil in October.
- We often use future time expressions such as ***tonight***, ***tomorrow***, ***this weekend***, ***this summer***, ***next week***, ***next month*** and ***after class/school***.
  What are you doing tonight?
  We're travelling to Paris this summer.
  Is he coming to the party on Saturday?

be going to

Affirmative		Negative	
I'm	going to run.	I'm not	going to run.
You're		You aren't	
He's		He isn't	
She's		She isn't	
It's		It isn't	
We're		We aren't	
You're		You aren't	
They're		They aren't	

- We use ***be going to*** to talk about future plans and intentions.
  She's going to take her camera on holiday.
  I'm going to wear my new trainers.
- To form the affirmative, we use ***be*** + ***going to*** + **infinitive**.
  We're going to have dinner in a restaurant.
- To form the negative, we use ***be*** + ***not*** + ***going to*** + **infinitive**. ***Not*** is usually contracted.
  They aren't going to go on holiday this summer.

Question	Short answer	
	Affirmative	Negative
Am I going to be there?	Yes, I am.	No, I'm not.
Are you going to be there?	Yes, you are.	No, you aren't.
Is he going to be there?	Yes, he is.	No, he isn't.
Is she going to be there?	Yes, she is.	No, she isn't.
Is it going to be there?	Yes, it is.	No, it isn't.
Are we going to be there?	Yes, we are.	No, we aren't.
Are you going to be there?	Yes, you are.	No, you aren't.
Are they going to be there?	Yes, they are.	No, they aren't.

- We form questions with ***be*** before the subject.
  Is he going to tell us the answers to the homework?
- We form information questions with a ***Wh-*** question word before ***be***.
  Who is he going to ask?
  What are you going to wear to the party?
  Why is Susana going to be late?

LANGUAGE PRACTICE UNIT 9

Future with *will/won't*

1 Complete the sentences about a camping trip. Write *'ll* or *won't*.

1 Don't sit at the bottom of the boat. You *'ll* ________ get wet.
2 Don't make the shelter. You ________ know how to do it.
3 Don't swim in the river. It's dangerous so you ________ be safe!
4 Don't eat and then swim. You ________ be sick!
5 Don't walk alone at night because you ________ get lost!
6 Don't lose your compass. You ________ know how to get back to the camp.

2 Write sentences with *will* or *won't* about the things you can do on holiday.

1 have a good time ✓ *I will have a good time.*
2 get bored ✗ ________
3 go to the beach every day ✓ ________
4 stay in a tent ✗ ________
5 eat good food ✓ ________
6 do any homework ✗ ________

Present continuous for future

3 Complete the email with the present continuous form of the verbs in brackets.

Hi Sandra,

How are you? It's the school holidays next week! I [1]*'m going* (go) on an adventure trip and my sister [2]________ (come) too! In August my dad [3]________ (take) me on a boat trip! My mum [4]________ (not go) because she doesn't like boats! She [5]________ (visit) my grandparents. I think you [6]________ (fly) to England for a week. Is that right? What are you doing after that?

Jorge

4 Complete the sentences with the present continuous form of the verbs in the box.

come go have ~~meet~~ not visit play

1 I'm *meeting* my friends tomorrow morning.
2 When ________ you ________ basketball?
3 ________ grandad ________ for lunch on Sunday?
4 ________ Ben and Sam ________ a party next week?
5 We ________ my aunt and uncle this weekend.
6 Where ________ you ________ shopping on Friday?

be going to

5 Rewrite the sentences in the negative.

1 I'm going to see my grandma next week.
I'm not going to see my grandma next week.
2 You are going to make new friends.
____
3 Marina is going to visit the wildlife park next month.
____
4 Mohammed is going to go to a summer camp next year.
____
5 We are going to learn how to make a shelter.
____
6 They are going to climb the mountain.
____

6 Complete the conversations with the correct form of *be going to*. Use the verbs in brackets.

1 **A:** *What are you going to do* (do) in the school holidays?
B: I ________ (visit) my aunt in London.

2 **A:** ________ (he / stay) in a hotel?
B: No, he ________

3 **A:** ________ (Gabriel and Ana / climb) in the mountains?
B: Yes, they ________

4 **A:** We ________ (not go) on holiday this year.
B: ________ (you / stay) at home?

LANGUAGE BANK

UNIT 4

Vocabulary

Food and drink

apples bananas beans carrots cheese
chicken chocolate eggs fish
fizzy drink juice meat rice water

Adjectives to describe food

cold delicious disgusting fresh healthy
hot nice salty sweet unhealthy

Language in action

Countable and uncountable nouns
a/an, some/any
there isn't/aren't
much, many, a lot of

Speaking

Everyday English

Enjoy!
Here you go.
No problem.
No worries!

Useful language

Can I have ... ?
Can I help you?
How much is that?
I'd like a/an/some ...
Is that everything?
That's ... , please.
What kind?
What's in the ... ?

Writing

Useful language

A description

We use *and* to add similar information.
We use *but* to contrast different information.
We use *or* when there is a choice (usually between two things).

UNIT 5

Vocabulary

Clothes

boots cap flip-flops hoodie jacket
jeans joggers shirt shorts
skirt T-shirt trainers

Accessories

belt bracelet earrings gloves necklace
purse ring scarf sunglasses umbrella
wallet watch

Language in action

Present continuous
Present simple and present continuous

Speaking

Everyday English

It's a bargain.
It's perfect.
No, honestly.
You're in luck!

Useful language

Can I help you?
Can I see the ... one, please?
Have you got it in a different (size/colour/style)?
I'm looking for ...
It comes in ...
What about this one / these?

Writing

Useful language

A description of a photo

at the back
in the middle
on the left/right
next to (someone)

LANGUAGE BANK

UNIT 6

Vocabulary

Sports

athletics basketball (mountain/rock) climbing gymnastics hockey rugby running sailing swimming table tennis volleyball windsurfing yoga

Sports verbs

bounce catch climb dive hit jump kick lift pass run score throw

Language in action

Comparatives
Superlatives

Speaking

Everyday English

Got them!
Look!
That's crazy!
What are we waiting for?
Why not?

Useful language

How much are tickets?
Let's book them.
Let's go.
Shall we go?
They're (£45).
What's the (quickest/best/cheapest) way to get there?

Writing

Useful language

A profile of a sportsperson

We use *also* and *too* to give extra information.
We use *also* after the verb *be*.
We use *also* before other verbs.
We use *too* at the end of a sentence.

UNIT 7

Vocabulary

Animals

Birds:
duck eagle parrot
Mammals:
bear donkey giraffe hippo horse lion monkey mouse whale
Reptiles:
crocodile snake

Adjectives

beautiful clever cute dangerous heavy huge large lazy light long noisy quiet safe short tiny wild

Language in action

was/were, there was/were
Past simple: regular and irregular verbs

Speaking

Everyday English

No way!
Really?
Wow!
You're joking!

Useful language

How was (the school trip)?
It was (really amazing).
What about (lions)?
What was (it) like?

Writing

Useful language

A biography

A few years ago
In 2007
On 10 October 2005

LANGUAGE BANK

UNIT 8

Vocabulary

Places in town

aquarium   bowling alley   car park
cinema   hospital   ice rink   post office
shopping centre   skate park   sports centre
swimming pool

Personal possessions

bus pass   camera   concert ticket   headphones
IC card   keys   laptop   money   passport
phone   portable charger   tablet

Grammar

Past simple: questions
Past simple: *Wh-* questions

Speaking

Everyday English

Calm down.
Don't panic!
Gross!
Let's drink.

Useful language

Did you have it when you (got to school)?
Did you put it (in your bag)?
What did you do with it after that?
When did you last (have/use/see) it?

Writing

Useful language

A blog post

I didn't hear my alarm **so** I got up late.

UNIT 9

Vocabulary

Outdoor life

use a compass   light a fire   read a map
build a shelter   catch a fish
find food and water   pick fruit
cook over a campfire   identify plants
collect wood

Holidays

apartment   bed & breakfast (B&B)
camper van   caravan   chalet   cottage
hotel   tent   youth hostel

Grammar

Future with *will/won't*
Present continuous for future
be going to

Speaking

Everyday English

Easy!
Forget that.
I'm on it!
You're unbelievable!

Useful language

What about a (film night)?
What are we going to do?
Why don't we (have a picnic)?
I'm not sure about that.
I'd rather not do that.
Let's do that!

Writing

Useful language

An email

at home
in the morning
in August
on Monday
on 1 August
at the airport

IRREGULAR VERBS

Infinitive	Past simple
be	was / were
beat	beat
become	became
begin	began
break	broke
bring	brought
build	built
buy	bought
catch	caught
choose	chose
come	came
cost	cost
cut	cut
do	did
draw	drew
drink	drank
drive	drove
eat	ate
fall	fell
feel	felt
fight	fought
find	found
fly	flew
forget	forgot
get	got
give	gave
go	went
grow	grew
have	had
hear	heard
hide	hid
hit	hit
hold	held
keep	kept

Infinitive	Past simple
know	knew
leave	left
lose	lost
make	made
meet	met
pay	paid
put	put
read	read
ride	rode
ring	rang
run	ran
say	said
see	saw
sell	sold
send	sent
show	showed
shut	shut
sing	sang
sit	sat
sleep	slept
speak	spoke
spend	spent
stand	stood
swim	swam
take	took
teach	taught
tell	told
think	thought
throw	threw
understand	understood
wake	woke
wear	wore
win	won
write	wrote

Student's Book acknowledgements

The authors and publishers acknowledge the following sources of copyright material and are grateful for the permissions granted. While every effort has been made, it has not always been possible to identify the sources of all the material used, or to trace all copyright holders. If any omissions are brought to our notice, we will be happy to include the appropriate acknowledgements on reprinting & in the next update to the digital edition, as applicable.

Key: FF = Fast Finishers, U = Unit, VB = Vocabulary Bank.

Photography

The following photographs are sourced from Getty Images.

U5: Jorge Fernández/LightRocket via Getty Images; Image Source/DigitalVision; yayayoyo/iStock/Getty Images Plus; davidcreacion/iStock/Getty Images Plus; Mochipet/iStock/Getty Images Plus; Andy Roberts/Caiaimage; ISMODE/iStock/Getty Images Plus; Sol de Zuasnabar Brebbia/Moment; lightasafeather/iStock/Getty Images Plus; s-cphoto/E+; Pongsak Tawansaeng/EyeEm; Ryan McVay/Photodisc; AndreyGorulko/iStock/Getty Images Plus; kenneth-cheung/E+; evemilla E+; pepifoto/E+; Saowakon Sukrak/EyeEm; malerapaso/iStock/Getty Images Plus; Steve Gorton/Dorling Kindersley; AnthonyRosenberg/iStock/Getty Images Plus; Fernando Trabanco Fotografía/Moment; Maria Taglienti-Molinari/Hulton Archive; Willowpix/E+; Juanmonino/E+; drbimages/E+; Echo/Juice Images; Cultura RM Exclusive/Stefano Gilera; Jbryson/iStock/Getty Images Plus; ImagesBazaar; Aaron Joel Santos/Aurora; tolgart/iStock/Getty Images Plus; transiastock/iStock/Getty Images Plus; Fgorgun/iStock/Getty Images Plus; Oleg Golovnev/EyeEm; mocoo/iStock/Getty Images Plus; **U6**: RyanJLane/E+; miki-tiger/iStock/Getty Images Plus; RapidEye/E+; ian600f/iStock/Getty Images Plus; Luka/Cultura; AAGAMIA/The Image Bank; Jon Feingersh/The Image Bank; Polhansen/iStock/Getty Images Plus; Westend61; kosmos111/kosmos111; PeopleImages/DigitalVision; Chris Cole/The Image Bank; Colin Bush/EyeEm; VisitBritain/Ben Selway; vinhdav/iStock/Getty Images Plus; NurPhoto/NurPhoto via Getty Images; Vladimir Godnik; Markus Gann/EyeEm; Ty Allison/Photographer's Choice; lzf/iStock/Getty Images Plus; Hero Images; somnuk krobkum/Moment; kevinruss/iStock/Getty Images Plus; MARC MUELLER/AFP/Getty Images; BRENDAN SMIALOWSKI/AFP/Getty Images; Keshav Singh/Hindustan Times via Getty Images; Klaus Vedfelt/DigitalVision; Lars Niki/Getty Images for The North Face; nenadpitarevic/iStock/Getty Images Plus; Nongluk Charoenpronwattanakun/EyeEm; 2e812ac3_768/iStock/Getty Images Plus; Don Mason; RunPhoto/Photodisc; mocoo/iStock/Getty Images Plus; Reinkefox/iStock/Getty Images Plus; **U7**: Inaki Relanzon/Nature Picture Library; Mostafa Gabr/EyeEm; Gerald & Buff Corsi/Visuals Unlimited; Dave Fleetham/Design Pics/Perspectives; Anup Shah/Stockbyte; Tim Platt/Stone; CreativeNature_nl/iStock/Getty Images Plus; Jeffrey Coolidge/DigitalVision; Barrie Thomas/EyeEm; Paul A. Souders/Corbis Documentary; ERNESTO BENAVIDES/AFP/Getty Images; Dorling Kindersley; Eric VANDEVILLE/Gamma-Rapho via Getty Images; A-Digit/DigitalVision Vectors; Jurgen & Christine Sohns; Jennifer Borton/DigitalVision Vectors; Fiona Davis/EyeEm; esancai/iStock/Getty Images Plus; John Crux Photography/Moment Open; baona/E+; Alan Tunnicliffe Photography/Moment; Tim Flach/Iconica; PomInOz/iStock/Getty Images Plus; Arun Roisri/Thailand; Jane Burton/Dorling Kindersley; GlobalP/iStock/Getty Images Plus; Barry Bland/Barcroft Media/Getty Images; guenterguni/E+; Adriano La Naia/EyeEm; Yuri_Arcurs/E+; TIMOTHY A. CLARY/AFP; Jeff R. Bottari/Getty Images Entertainment; Barcroft Media; Paul Souders/Corbis Documentary; Ysanne Slide/Moviestore collection Ltd/Alamy Stock Photo; Serjio74/iStock/Getty Images Plus; Kauriana/iStock/Getty Images Plus; ChrisGorgio/iStock/Getty Images Plus; krugli/iStock/Getty Images Plus; perysty/iStock/Getty Images Plus; Ace_Create/DigitalVision Vectors; Fabian Berg/EyeEm; JuliarStudio/iStock/Getty Images Plus; luplupme/iStock/Getty Images Plus; mocoo/iStock/Getty Images Plus; Eg Project/Photonica; Walter Zerla/Blend Images; Maremagnum/Photodisc; wakila/E+; Streeter Lecka/Getty Images; alxpin/iStock/Getty Images Plus; kevinjeon00/E+; Jon Shireman/Photonica; ihoe/iStock/Getty Images Plus; Vostok/Moment & Vostok/Moment; Jon Hicks/Corbis Documentary; Spaces Images/Blend Images; Yongyuan Dai/The Image Bank; Science Picture Co/Collection Mix: Subjects; Dmitry Berkut/iStock/Getty Images Plus; ENRIQUE MARCARIAN/REUTERS/Newscom; Hemant Mehta; **U8**: David De Lossy/Valueline/Getty Images Plus; Richard Boll/Photographer's Choice; Scoobers/iStock Editorial/Getty Images Plus; daizuoxin/iStock/Getty Images Plus; Zerbor/iStock/Getty Images Plus; Tetra Images; Ryan McVay/Photodisc; pbombaert/Moment; Nick Dolding/The Image Bank; j_markow/iStock/Getty Images Plus; rasikabendre/iStock/Getty Images Plus; s-cphoto/E+; Bloom Productions/Taxi; pixelfusion3d/iStock/Getty Images Plus; jashlock/iStock/Getty Images Plus; ti-ja/iStock/Getty Images Plus; Haywood Magee/Picture Post/Hulton Archive/Getty Images; Steve Heap/Canopy; Folb/Topical Press Agency/Getty Images; Igor Golovniov/EyeEm; oxygen/Moment; Pinghung Chen/EyeEm; oxygen/Moment; George Marks/Retrofile RF; damircudic/E+; PeopleImages/E+; oxygen/Moment; Hybrid Images/Cultura; mocoo/iStock/Getty Images Plus; **U9**: Shing Chak Wong/EyeEm; Eye Ubiquitous/UIG via Getty Images; David De Lossy/Photodisc; ©Studio One-One/Moment Open; Burak Karademir/Moment; Ismailciydem/iStock/Getty Images Plus; Diana Mayfield/Lonely Planet Images; Caiaimage/Chris Newton; Westend61; DarthArt/iStock Editorial/Getty Images Plus; Simon Watson/The Image Bank; Photawa/iStock Editorial/Getty Images Plus; Billy Currie Photography/Moment; HAGENMULLER Jean-Francois/Hemis.fr; ewg3D/iStock/Getty Images Plus; monkeybusinessimages/iStock/Getty Images Plus; SeventyFour/iStock/Getty Images Plus; Stephen Spraggon/Photolibrary; Hero Images; KatarzynaBialasiewicz/iStock/Getty Images Plus; Hill Street Studios/Blend Images; John Giustina/Iconica; abishome/iStock/Getty Images Plus; Hero Images; Ariel Skelley/DigitalVision; Letizia Le Fur/ONOKY; Inti St. Clair, Inc; ozgurdonmaz/iStock/Getty Images Plus; BrankoPhoto/iStock/Getty Images Plus; mocoo/iStock/Getty Images Plus; **FF5**: Westend61; Ronnie Kaufman/DigitalVision; Roy JAMES Shakespeare/Photodisc; Gpointstudio/Cultura; **FF7**: nicolamargaret/iStock/Getty Images Plus; Audrey Saracco/EyeEm; acceptfoto/iStock/Getty Images Plus; mmozzies/iStock/Getty Images Plus; Tier Und Naturfotografie J und C Sohns/Photographer's Choice; Rob Lind/EyeEm; Vicki Jauron, Babylon and Beyond Photography/Moment;PILLAIBALANMADHAVAN/iStock/Getty Images Plus;Moiz_Cukurel/iStock/Getty Images Plus;claudialothering/RooM; **FF8**: skynesher/E+; Denny Soetiono/EyeEm; Stella; Михаил Руденко/iStock/Getty Images Plus; Sorapong Chaipanya/EyeEm; Rondeau Laetitia/EyeEm; Raphael Brian Espineli/EyeEm; baona/iStock/Getty Images Plus; Jasmin Merdan/Moment; Image Source/Image Source; yulkapopkova/iStock/Getty Images Plus; **FF9**: summerphotos/iStock/Getty Images Plus; **VB5**: Nophamon Yanyapong/EyeEm; Radionphoto/iStock/Getty Images Plus; clu/E+; NAKphotos/iStock/Getty Images Plus; mattiestudio/iStock/Getty Images Plus; Issaurinko/iStock/Getty Images Plus; malerapaso/iStock/Getty Images Plus; OxfordSquare/iStock/Getty Images Plus; akova/iStock/Getty Images Plus; mawielobob/iStock/Getty Images Plus; ersinkisacik/iStock/Getty Images Plus; Ng Sok Lian/EyeEm; **VB6**: baona/iStock/Getty Images Plus; Vedrana Sucic/EyeEm; Steve Smith; Patrik Giardino/Corbis; Joe Patronite/The Image Bank; Alistair Berg/DigitalVision; PeopleImages/E+; Marc Princivalle for imagesconcept.com/Moment; Peter Noyce/LOOP IMAGES/Corbis Documentary; Aksonov/E+; Mike Kemp;Johner Images; Andrii Afanasiev/EyeEm; **VB7**: Andrea Croati/EyeEm; Kryssia Campos/Moment; sjharmon/E+; Chris Beavon/Moment; Jim Adams/500px; Jens Huelsmeier/EyeEm; Joe McDonald/Corbis Documentary; Travelographer 1/500px; Vicki Jauron, Babylon and Beyond Photography/Moment; Images from BarbAnna/Moment; silversaltphoto.j.senosiain/Moment Open; Ultima_Gaina/iStock/Getty Images Plus;Ryan Petersen/EyeEm; Tim Melling/Moment; **VB8**: damircudic/E+; tma1/E+; Aliraza Khatri's Photography/Moment; Steve Debenport/iStock/Getty Images Plus; SimplyCreativePhotography/E+; Billy Hustace/The Image Bank; Oleksiy Maksymenko/All Canada Photos; Westend61; shank_ali/E+; Nongnuch Leelaphasuk/EyeEm; cscredon/E+; **VB9**: Toby Howard/Moment; photo by Chris Axe/Moment; Peter John Dickson/Moment Mobile; Vadim Sushchenko/iStock/Getty Images Plus; juhy13/E+; Geography Photos/Universal Images Group;buzbuzzer/iStock; Yuriy_Kulik/iStock/Getty Images Plus; DaveLongMedia/E+; **CLIL6**: TREVOR JOHNSTON/Eye Meets World Photography; QAI Publishing/UIG via Getty Images; Hero Images/DigitalVision; **CLIL8**: Ralph Morse/The LIFE Premium Collection/Getty Images; Universal History Archive/UIG via Getty Images; stellalevi/iStock/Getty Images Plus.

The following photographs are sourced from other libraries/sources.

U5, U8: Carboxylase/Shutterstock; **U8:** ENRIQUE MARCARIAN/REUTERS/Newscom; **ICONS:** Prithvi/Noun Project; Agni/Noun Project; mikicon/Noun Project; Baboon designs, US/Noun Project; Tanguy Keryhuel, FR/Noun Project; Icons Bazaar/Noun Project; Adrien Coquet, FR/Noun Project; Vectors Market/Noun Project; TukTuk Design/Noun Project; iconsphere, ID/Noun Project; i cons, US/Noun Project; kim Eriksson/Noun Project; Lloyd Humphreys, DK/Noun Project; Delwar Hossain, BD/Noun Project; Kirby Wu, TW/Noun Project; Magicon, HU/Noun Project; Baboon designs, US/Noun Project.

Video Stills

U5: monkeybusinessimages/Creatas Video+/Getty Images Plus; Yellow Dog Productions Inc./Image Bank Film: Signature; **U6**: 3sbworld/Creatas Video+/Getty Images Plus; **U7**: Mark Kostich/Creatas Video; DDCoral/Creatas Video+/Getty Images Plus; **U8**: HeroImagesFootage/Creatas Video; **U9**: Faithfulshot/DigitalVision; LeoPatrizi/Vetta.

Illustration

U5: Alex Herrerías; Chelen Écija; Antonio Cuesta Cornejo; Mark Duffin; **U6**: Chelen Écija; **U7**: Mark Duffin; **U8**: Alex Herrerías; Chelen Écija; Mark Duffin; **U9**: Alex Herrerías; Chelen Écija; **CLIL6**: Alex Herrerías.

Cover design and illustrations: Collaborate Agency.

Video production by Lucentum Digital.

Audio production by Creative Listening.

Typeset by Blooberry Design.